The tsunami celebrity cookbook

favourite food
from
FAMOUS FACES

Compiled by Brigette Hardy and Sarah Jefferies

First published in Great Britain 2005 by PMDC
Printed and bound by CPI, Bath

Recipes © Individual Contributors 2005
Compilation © Brigette Hardy, Sarah Jefferies 2005
Design © The Paul Martin Design Company Ltd 2005

A CIP catalogue record of this book is available from
the British Library.

ISBN: 0 9551983 0 5

The publishers have made every effort to assign the
correct copyright to all contributors and apologise for
any omissions or errors.

Brigette Hardy and Sarah Jefferies have made every
effort to obtain full approval, formal agreement,
photographer credits and permissions from contributors
and publishers before going to print and apologise for
any unintentional omissions or details not corrected or
received before this date.

The Paul Martin Design **Company**

The tsunami celebrity cookbook

favourite food
from
FAMOUS FACES

Compiled by Brigette Hardy and Sarah Jefferies

Foreword

I am greatly pleased to have been asked to dedicate
this book in memory of members of my family and
their close friends who tragically died in the Tsunami
on December 26th 2004. The group of six friends
were staying by the beach in Khao Lak, which was the
worst hit place in Thailand.

May I thank the friends of those who died who
have given their time to producing this book, the
celebrities and others who kindly contributed their
favourite recipes and, of course, the Paul Martin
design team who have so generously donated their
services. All the proceeds will go directly to the Khao
Lak Community Appeal, a charity set up in memory
of the six who died. The charity is raising funds for
new buildings and facilities at the Khao Lak School
and to sponsor the education of 11 children known to
the group who lost one or more of their parents.

And lastly, may I take this opportunity to thank
everyone for supporting the charity by buying copies
of this book.

Lord Attenborough

for Melanie Clough, Lucy Elizabeth Holland, Jane Mary Holland,
(Audrey) Jane Holland, Pippa Rea & Holly Riddle

The Khao Lak Community Appeal

The Khao Lak Community Appeal was launched in January 2005 in memory
of six friends who died in the tragic events of the Tsunami on Boxing Day 26th
December 2004. They were holidaying in Khao Lak, the most devastated area in
Thailand. The charity is also in recognition of the fantastic people of Khao Lak,
who did so much to help survivors, having lost virtually everything themselves.

Khao Lak is situated on the mainland west coast of Thailand, sixty kilometres
north of Phuket Island. It is a community which has existed around the fishing and
farming industry and, in more recent years has started to develop tourism.

The village was torn apart by the Tsunami. From a population of around 25,000
people over 5,000 including tourists died in Khao Lak. No family remained
untouched by the events, livelihoods were decimated, homes, hotels, shops,
restaurants, fishing boats and dive centres were literally washed away.

The Appeal aims to raise £1 million to build new and improve existing facilities at
the local school and for community use as well. It will also support eleven young
children throughout their schooling, all of whom lost their mothers in the wave.

The Khao Lak Community Appeal will use the funds to:

- Build a language and IT laboratory.
- Provide ongoing English language teaching staff from Dulwich College
  in Phuket (affiliated to Dulwich College, London).
- Build a swimming pool and provide a swimming teacher –
  many Thai people died in the wave because they could not swim.
- Improve staff accommodation and school toilet facilities.
- Provide a park area and, subject to future funds a football pitch.

Most importantly the charity recognises the importance of providing ongoing
funds so that the facilities will be able to operate and be enjoyed by future
generations of the Khao Lak community. This will be provided by investment of
the remainder of the funds raised.

www.khaolakappeal.com.

starters

Cockles	135
Crab & Sweetcorn Spring Rolls	82
Cold Terrine of Hardboiled Eggs	94
Pickled Egg on a Doily	106
Grilled Prawns with Tomato & Basil Butter	74
Prawn Dish	45
Crunchy Thai Wraps	98
Chicken and Roasted Pepper Soup	41
Clear Thai Salmon & Lobster Soup	83
Emsworth Cockle & Crab Chowder	29
Gazpacho Andaluz	146
Miso Stew	7
Pippa's Mushroom Soup	105
Salmon Chowder	72
Scottish Highland Kick	116
Sebag's Special Moroccan Lentil Soup	120
Spinach Soup	94
Veggie Soup	84

main

BEEF

Beef Casserole	69
Chilli Mince Taco	110
Fabada	49
Spicy Shepherd's Pie	102
Meat Loaf wrapped in Bacon	6
Pie & Mash	126
Corned Beef Hash	14

CHICKEN/POULTRY

Chicken (or Turkey) Boobs	73
Cheat's Chicken	136
Chicken Casserole	59
Chicken Marbella	15
Guidwife Chicken	30
Khao Soi	38
Portuguese Chicken with Roasted Vegetable Ratatouille	4
Poulet St. Barth	85
Poussin	16
Surprise Chicken in a Parcel	36
Swiss Chicken Ham Bake	17
Thai Chicken Cakes with Sweet Chilli Sauce	81
Thai Green Curry with Chicken	122
Little Thai Chicken Recipe	47
Thai Green Curry Paste	67
Thai Chicken Curry	57
Wok Fried Basil & Chilli Chicken	54

main

LAMB

Fred's Lamb Curry	35
Lamb Cutlets Shrewsbury	131
Bhuna Gosht (Pan Roasted Lamb)	87
Rack of Lamb with Beans & Roasted Onions	70

PORK

Egg and Bacon Croquettes	11
Mark's Cajun Pork	62
Sausage & Cabbage Casserole	107
Venison Sausages Braised in Red Wine	128

FISH

Crayfish & Avocado Sandwich	9
Creamy Fish Pie	12
Fish Fingers, Chips and Beans	44
Thai Fish Cakes / Thai Dipping Sauce	142
Smoked Haddock Balls	92
Loin of Monkfish Stuffed with Basil Sunblush Tomato & Mozzarella	124
Monkfish in Filo Pastry with Red Onion	18
Monkfish, Prawns & Mushrooms in a Lime and Dill Sauce	78
Red Mullet, Tomato Risotto, Basil Oil	39
Moslem-style Curry with Mushrooms & Prawns	23
Moslem-style Curry Paste	22
Thai Marinated Steamed Salmon	96
Seared Scallops with Mixed Salad Leaves	71
Thai-baked Sea Bass with Fragrant Rice	10
Grilled Seabream with Pistou of Shellfish	75

rice, pasta, vegetables

Pasta with Broccoli & Pinenuts	134
Pasta with Cheese & Peanut Sauce	108
Tom's Cheesy Pasta	77
Chicken Pasta	111
Griddled Chicken Pasta with Spinach & Parmesan	65
Isabella 'Master Chef' Chickpea Pasta	56
Over-Indulgent Pasta	103
Ceejay's Hot Roasted Salmon & Pasta	63
Pasta al Tonno	33
Spaghetti aur Machli Roberto Silvi	86
Creamy Vegetable Lasagne	93
Bangkok Street Noodles	24
Thai Prawn Noodles	133
Spiced Lentil Salsa	28
Vegetarian Paella	48
Brown Rice & Chinese Style Vegetables	90
Thai Roasted Crab Risotto	80
Prawn and Asparagus Risotto	52
Beans à la Clarkson	27
Cauliflower from Amalfi	40
Champ	60
My Mum's Potato Cakes	117
Jacket Potato	140
Rosemary Potatoes	68
Roasted Tomato & Goats' Cheese Tart with Thyme	64
Stir Fry Fresh Vegetables	77
Vegetable Kadai	113

salad

A Slimmer's Lunch 51

Char Grilled Thai Beef Salad 144

Fragrant Beef Salad with Grapes 20

Magic Paste 21

Chicken & Mango Salad 61

Thai Green Apple Salad 8

Thai Watermelon Salad 99

Vietnamese Salad 50

desserts

Apple Crumble 66

Bread & Butter Pudding 34

Chocolate Brandy Whip 112

Delicious Pudding 137

Dulce De Leche Soufflé 119

Grandpa's Cheat 92

Infallible Ice Cream 125

Malva Pudding 19

Sliced Mango with Greek Yoghurt 107

Mars Bar Chop 43

Pancakes De Dulce De Leche 118

Peaches & Pears in Wine 58

Pear, Chocolate & Frangipan Strudel with Vanilla Ice Cream 130

Pimms Jelly 139

'Quartet' Fruit Salad 88

Ricotta Cheese Cake with Limoncello Liquer and Marinated Strawberries 95

Strawberries & Lemon Curd with Filo Pastry 76

Iced Strawberry Parfait with Malibu Salsa 104

baking

Chocolate Brownies 141

Tara P-T's Chocolate Crispies 101

Ginger Biscuits 138

Lavender Shortbread 26

Mum's Oat Cookies 46

My Mum's Shortbread 79

Apple & Rosemary Cake 42

Banana Cake 145

Guinness Cake 32

Moll's Marmalade Cake 100

Planter's Punch 132

Jane Asher

PORTUGUESE CHICKEN WITH ROASTED VEGETABLE RATATOUILLE

Ingredients for the Portuguese Chicken

4 skinless chicken breasts
2 tablespoons runny honey
2 tablespoons lemon juice
2 teaspoons tomato puree
1 level teaspoon Piri-Piri seasoning

Ingredients for the Ratatouille

225g (8 oz) aubergines – halved and diced
2 large courgettes – diced
2 red peppers – de-seeded and cut into strips
2 red onions – cut in quarters
6 plum tomatoes – cut into 4
2 cloves of garlic – peeled and crushed
2 sweet potatoes – orange flesh – peeled and diced
2 sprigs of fresh thyme
2 sprigs of fresh basil leaves
50ml (2 fl oz) olive oil
225 g (8 oz) passata (or tin of peeled chopped tomatoes)
salt and pepper

Portuguese Chicken

Mix together the honey, lemon juice, tomato puree and piri-piri seasoning. Place the chicken pieces in a shallow dish and pour over the marinade. Leave overnight if possible.
N.B. You may want to slash the surface of the chicken breasts if you don't have much time to marinade. Place the chicken in a shallow roasting dish or a tin, and bake for 30–40 minutes at 180°C / 350°F / Gas mark 4 brushing the chicken with the marinade from time to time.

Ratatouille

Place the peeled and diced sweet potatoes in a pan, bring to the boil and cook for approximately 5 minutes. Drain and refresh in cold water. Place in a roasting tin with the garlic and thyme. Add the rest of the prepared vegetables, drizzle with olive oil and season. Roast the vegetables at 200°C / 400°F / Gas mark 6 for 40–45 minutes or until golden brown. Bring the passata to the boil and pour over the vegetables. Place back in the oven for a further 10 minutes until bubbling and hot.

Serve the chicken with a portion of the ratatouille, garnished with torn basil leaves.

Serves 4   Prep time: 30 minutes   Cooking time: 1 hour   495 calories per serving

Jane Asher is well known for her acting, writing and her cakes. She has been acting since she was 5 years old and has appeared in many famous film, television and theatre productions. She is currently at the Royal Court Theatre starring in *The World's Biggest Diamond*. She has written 3 best selling novels and more than a dozen lifestyle and cake decorating books. Her latest book is *Cakes for Fun*. Her cake company was set up 1990 and has become the UK's foremost bespoke cake decorating company.

George Baker
MEAT LOAF wrapped in BACON

2 small onions
1 clove garlic
2 teaspoons capers
1 tablespoon chopped mint
1 tablespoon chopped parsley
1 teaspoon chopped dill
1 teaspoon chopped basil
800g (1¾ lb) best mince
1 teaspoon mustard
2 lemons
Salt and freshly ground black pepper
225g (8 oz) long back bacon

Peel the onions and chop with garlic, capers and herbs in a food blender.
Put the mince into a bowl and mix the chopped ingredients with it. Add the mustard and the juice of one lemon, season with salt and pepper.

Preheat the oven to 190°C / 375°F / Gas mark 5. Cut the rind from the bacon, take a good sized piece of foil, line with a sheet of greaseproof paper and lay upon it the bacon, arranging it thin-end to thick-end alternately to cover the greaseproof.

Shape the meat into a loaf, stand it on the bacon strips and wrap them round it.

Cut the remaining lemon into quarters and arrange it round the loaf.
Wrap the foil round the meat and the lemon quarters, and put it into a loaf tin.

Bake for around 30–35 minutes.

Serve with crusty bread.

George Baker is
the star of, among many other
productions, the *Inspector Wexford*
series of television thrillers which is currently
showing on satellite television. He is one of
the acting business's most famous cooks.
This recipe comes from his cookbook, *A
Cook For All Seasons*, published by
Boxtree.

Nicola Beauman
MISO STEW

Nicola Beauman founded
Persephone books in 1999. Its books
are for, by and about women.

*There is no rational reason why people in the west eat dairy
produce, eggs and wheat, with possibly some fruit, for breakfast
- this is just a habit, and a profitable one for cereal and dairy
manufacturers. It would be far, far better if we ate vegetables. But,
it is true, a salad does not really hit the spot in the morning. I suggest the following,
which is easy, delicious, incredibly healthy, just somewhat unconventional in the west:*

*Fry a small onion in olive oil, add a few florets of broccoli, a sliced carrot, a sliced
stick of celery etc (by etc I mean whatever you have, e.g. a head of chicory, some
cabbage, some green beans). Cook for a minute and add a couple of cups of water.
Bring to the boil and remove from heat. If you like, add a handful of frozen peas,
ditto of chopped parsley, some cooked brown rice or quinoa, a little bit of chopped
tofu. Take it off the boil. Add a tablespoon of miso (this is an incredibly nourishing
flavouring, a cross between soya sauce and gravy, which has every important nutrient
known to man and is delicious; it should not be added to boiling water or the healthy
nutrients are destroyed.) I sometimes add some chopped lettuce at the last moment,
it seems extravagant to cook lettuce as it all but vanishes but it is so good. This is
my favourite breakfast. But you can't eat it in front of other people as they think it
is so ODD. N.B. Alas, you can only buy miso and quinoa in health-food shops. I
say alas because the bizarre conventions whereby you are allowed to buy some food
in some shops and others in another is one of the things that makes modern life so
complicated. (Quinoa is another new discovery, very, very nourishing - it's the staple
in South America - and very easy to cook, i.e. one cup of quinoa to two cups of water
cooked for ten minutes, quicker to cook than brown rice and less bland.)*

Very best wishes

Nicola

7

Fiona Beckett
THAI GREEN APPLE SALAD

One of my favourite salads is Thai green papaya salad but papayas are hard to get hold of in this country and are expensive when you do. This is a version I invented for my vegetarian student cookbook 'Beyond Baked Beans Green', which tastes just as good and is deliciously refreshing.

Serves 4 or 6 with other dishes.

150g unsalted, roasted peanuts in the shell (monkey nuts)
Juice of 1 large lemon
2 medium to large Granny Smith apples
1 large carrot
2 spring onions, trimmed and finely sliced
1 clove of garlic, peeled and crushed
1 mild green or red chilli, de-seeded and finely chopped
2 tablespoons light soy sauce
2 teaspoon golden caster sugar
½ teaspoon Thai chilli jam (optional)
4-5 mint leaves, very finely chopped
2 tablespoons chopped fresh coriander leaves
Salt or extra lemon juice to taste

Fiona Beckett is a renowned food and drink writer who specializes in food and drink matching. She has written for most of the broadsheets including *The Times, Telegraph* and *The Guardian,* and for specialist food and wine magazines such as *Decanter, Sainsbury's Magazine, BBC Good Food, Waitrose Food Illustrated, Bon Appetit* and *Australian Gourmet Traveller.* In 2002 she was voted Food Journalist of the year by the British Guild of Food Writers. She currently writes for *The Financial Times.*

Shell the peanuts (you should get about 50g of shelled nuts), rub off as much of the papery skins as possible and chop the nuts roughly. Put the lemon juice in a bowl. Quarter the apples and chop into short, thin strips, mixing it with the lemon juice as you go so that it doesn't brown. Peel and cut the carrot into similar sized strips and add to the apple along with the sliced spring onions, crushed garlic and chopped chilli. Mix the soy sauce with the sugar and chilli jam, (if using), and pour over the salad. Add the chopped peanuts, mint and coriander leaves and toss together. Check the seasoning, adding more lemon juice and/or a little salt if you think it needs it.

If you can't find whole peanuts in the shell use shelled, unsalted peanuts and toast them in a dry frying pan until the skins begin to turn brown. Set aside to cool then rub off the papery skins as above.

WARNING: Do not give this dish to anyone without checking whether they are allergic to peanuts.

From Fiona Beckett's vegetarian student cookbook *Beyond Baked Beans Green* published by Absolute Press.

Sinclair Beecham
CRAYFISH & AVOCADO SANDWICH

2 slices of good, fresh unbuttered granary or brown bread
½ perfectly ripe avocado
1 tablespoon of home made Marie-Rose sauce
half cup of peeled crayfish tails
¼ lemon
1 small pinch of paprika
sea salt and coarse-ground black pepper
mixed lettuce leaves

Sinclair Beecham co-founded *Pret-a-Manger* in 1986 having spotted a previously unexploited niche in the market – fresh, nutritious food 'on the go'. The time was right to reinvent the sandwich – or at least jazz it up. Eighteen years on, both Sinclair and his business partner boast MBEs and the sandwich has never been seen in the same light since. Sinclair lives with his sons and girlfriend in Hampshire.

Preparing the filling

1. It is hard to get hold of good crayfish. If you can't get crayfish, use three or four fat Tiger Prawns (cooked). Put them in a bowl and squeeze the lemon juice over them. Dust with paprika.

2. Find a ripe avocado, cut in half lengthways and pop the stone out with a spoon. Peel and slice.

3. To make Marie-Rose sauce, mix a tablespoon of mayonnaise with one of Heinz Tomato Ketchup. Season with Worcester Sauce, sea salt and black pepper.

Making the sandwich

1. Spread a tablespoon of home made Marie-Rose sauce on the bread.

2. Cover with slices of avocado, arranged edge to edge so that nearly all the bread is hidden.

3. Scatter the crayfish on top.

4. Season with sea salt and coarse ground pepper.

5. Cover with plenty of lettuce and rocket.

6. Put the second slice of bread on the top and cut in half diagonally with a sharp knife.

Alan Bird – Head Chef at the Ivy Restaurant
THAI-BAKED SEA BASS
with FRAGRANT RICE

You can sometimes order banana leaves from a good Asian or exotic greengrocer. If that fails wrap the fish in foil or greaseproof paper.

for the dipping sauce

25 ml sesame oil
1 small red chilli, de-seeded and finely chopped
35g ginger, peeled and finely chopped
1 stick lemon grass
3 lime leaves
2 cloves garlic, peeled and crushed
125 ml sweet soy sauce
100 ml light soy sauce

for the fragrant rice

2 sticks lemon grass, bulbous ends crushed
8 lime leaves
salt
1.5 litre water
225g basmati rice, washed twice in cold water

for the Sea Bass

35 ml sesame oil
3 medium chillies, de-seeded and roughly chopped
3 sticks lemon grass, peeled and bulbous ends roughly chopped
80g root ginger or galangal, peeled and roughly chopped
4 cloves garlic, peeled and crushed
8 lime leaves, roughly chopped
15g coriander
8 x 200g pieces Sea Bass, scaled and filleted
1–2 metres banana leaf

First, make the dipping sauce. Heat the sesame oil in a pan and fry the chilli, ginger, lemon grass and lime leaves slowly with the garlic for 1 minute to soften and release the flavours. Add both soy sauces, bring the mixture to the boil, then cool and pour it into a bowl or, ideally, individual soy dishes.

Now for the rice: simmer the lemon grass with the lime leaves in 1.5 litres salted water for 10 minutes. Add the rice and simmer it for 10–12 minutes until it is just cooked. Drain in a colander, then return it to the pan with a lid on, and let it stand for 10 minutes before serving. This will help it become nice and fluffy. Serve the rice in individual bowls or put it in a large bowl to pass around to guests.

While the rice is cooking, prepare the fish. Heat the sesame oil in a pan and fry the chillies, lemon grass, ginger, garlic and lime leaves in it for a couple of minutes. Then put them into a food processor with the coriander and chop them finely. Preheat the oven to 200°C / 400°F / Gas mark 6. Spread the paste on each fillet and wrap it in a piece of banana leaf like a parcel, folding the leaf so that the edges join underneath the fillet. Bake for 10–15 minutes. Serve the fish on individual plates with a little pot of dipping sauce and either individual bowls of fragrant rice or pass a large bowl round.

Mark Birley
EGG & BACON CROQUETTES

ingredients (makes about 14 large croquettes)

6 hard boiled eggs, chopped
250g (9 oz) of streaky bacon
3 tablespoons of chopped parsley
¼ teaspoon of ground nutmeg
3 leaves of gelatine

for the Chicken Veloute

570ml (1 pint) of chicken stock
25g (1 oz) of unsalted butter
50g (2 oz) of plain flour

for the egg wash and crumb

2 egg yolks
425ml (¾ of pint) of milk
75g (3oz) plain flour (seasoned)
bread crumbs

Connoisseur, arbiter, and de-facto protector of taste and quality in all matters relating to style-of-life. Standard-bearer for those aspiring to the zenith of good living, Mark is a legend in his field to both billionaire and pauper alike.

Founder of London-based *Annabels*, *Mark's Club*, *Harry's Bar*, *The George Club* and *The Bath and Racquet Club*.

Firstly prepare the veloute:

Place the butter in a warm saucepan until it is melted. Slowly add plain flour blending it together whilst cooking it slowly. Once the roux is cooked gently add the chicken stock mixing it until it is smooth (but not brown).

Meanwhile grill the bacon until crispy, then chop into small pieces.

Add the chopped hard boiled eggs and the chopped bacon to the veloute mixing it all together. Add three leaves of gelatine to the mixture and finally the chopped parsley and ground nutmeg. N.B. There is no need to add any extra salt as the bacon is salty enough as is. Add pepper to taste.

Place the mixture on a flat tray and spread it out, covering with some buttered greaseproof paper and leave until cold.

Whisk the egg yolk and milk together to make an egg wash.

Remove the cold mixture from the tray and place into a bowl, giving it a stir. Make small croquette shapes out of the mixture, rolling them in seasoned flour then the egg wash and then the bread crumbs.

Fry the croquettes until golden and serve with fried English parsley.

Roger Black MBE
CREAMY FISH PIE

Serves 4

1kg large floury potatoes, eg. Maris Piper, peeled and cut into chunks
25g butter
1 tablespoon olive oil
2 cloves garlic, crushed
550g natural boneless and skinless prime cod or haddock fillets
150g natural boneless Scottish smoked haddock fillets, skinned and cut into large pieces
2 teaspoons mustard
500ml tub half fat crème fraîche
1 x 20g pack fresh flat-leaf parsley, chopped

Cook the potatoes in boiling water for 15–20 minutes until tender. While the potatoes are cooking, heat the butter, olive oil and garlic in a large, non-stick frying pan until the butter begins to foam. Over a high heat, fry the fish pieces in batches for 1–2 minutes on each side. Remove the pieces when cooked and keep warm on a plate. Return the fish to the pan when it is all cooked.

Spoon the mustard, crème fraîche and parsley over the fish, allowing the mixture to melt into the fish without stirring – it will look quite liquified at this stage. Preheat the grill to high.

Drain the cooked potatoes thoroughly. Add 4 tbsp of the creamy fish liquid and mash until smooth and creamy. Spoon the mashed potato roughly over the fish. It does not matter if some of the mash drops to the bottom of the pan, rather than sitting on top.

Place the pan under the hot grill for 3–5 minutes until the potato is golden. Serve immediately with broccoli, peas or spinach.

Variation: The cooked fish can be spooned over hot baked potatoes or eaten with nutty brown rice.

This recipe is quick and easy and fish is so good for you.

Wishing you every success with the fund raising.

Roger Black MBE

For fourteen years Roger Black represented Great Britain at the highest level in the world of athletics, both as an individual 400 metres runner and as a member of the 4x400 metres relay team. He won fifteen major Championship medals including European, Commonwealth and World Championship Gold medals. His greatest achievement was winning the Olympic 400 metres Silver medal in 1996. He was British Men's Team Captain and was awarded the MBE in 1992. Roger Black is now a television presenter and an accomplished motivational speaker and conference host. He is also not a bad dancer!

Sir Peter & Lady Pippa Blake
CORNED BEEF HASH

Peter's favourite recipe at sea was corned beef hash - i.e. mashed potato, corned beef and onions mashed together and fried up.

In over 40 years of sailing, New Zealander, Sir Peter Blake competed in five Whitbread Round- the-World Races, winning in 1989/90 on board 'Steinlager 2'. In 1994 he won the Jules Verne Trophy with a record-breaking non-stop voyage on ENZA, and then went on to his greatest achievement in 1995 winning the Americas Cup for New Zealand.

In 1995, he was knighted by the Queen for his services to the sport of sailing.

In 2000, Sir Peter formed 'Blake Expeditions' with the aim of educating and encouraging people to protect life in, on and around the sea in those parts of the world, which are key to the planets ecosystem. It was on Sir Peter's second voyage on 'Seamaster' in the Amazon that he was tragically killed by pirates.

In November 2002, the late Sir Peter Blake was honoured by the International Olympic Committee with the presentation by His Majesty King Constantine of the IOC Olympic Order, which was accepted by Lady Pippa Blake on her late husband's behalf. This took place at Emsworth Sailing Club.

This recipe was given by Lady Pippa Blake as it was Sir Peter's favourite recipe whilst at sea.

Lady Pippa Blake
CHICKEN MARBELLA

For entertaining at home or, if the ingredients were available, cruising with family and friends. A favourite recipe was and still is, Chicken Marbella from an American cookbook.

Quantities for 10–12

10/12 boned chicken breasts or large thighs
1 head of garlic, peeled and chopped
¼ cup dried oregano
coarse salt and fresh ground black pepper
½ cup red wine vinegar
½ cup olive oil
1 cup pitted prunes
½ cup pitted green olives
½ cup capers with a bit of juice
6 bay leaves
1 cup brown sugar
1 cup white wine
¼ cup chopped fresh parsley or coriander

1. In a large bowl combine chicken pieces, garlic, oregano, pepper and salt to taste, vinegar, olive oil, prunes, olives, capers and juice and bay leaves. Cover and marinate, refrigerated, overnight.

2. Preheat oven to 180°C / 350°F / Gas mark 4.

3. Arrange chicken pieces in a single layer in one or two large shallow baking pans and spoon marinade over evenly. Sprinkle chicken pieces with brown sugar and pour white wine around them.

4. Bake for 50 minutes to 1 hour, basting frequently with pan juices until the chicken is cooked.

5. With a slotted spoon transfer the chicken, prunes and capers to a serving platter. Moisten with a few spoonfuls of pan juices and sprinkle generously with parley or coriander.

6. Chicken Marbella is also very good served cold. Allow to return to room temperature before serving.

Lady Pippa Blake studied Fine Art at Camberwell School of Art in London, gaining a First Class BA Honours degree in painting. She went to work for the Arts Council of Great Britain and as an assistant to a Museum Designer based in Chelsea, London.

Pippa and Peter Blake were married in August 1979, their first adventure followed with a three month journey to Sydney to deliver the yacht Condor of Bermuda for the Sydney Hobart race 1979. They then moved on to New Zealand where Pippa worked in the organisation and liaison for Ceramco NZ and many subsequent races and expeditions.

In 1993 Pippa resumed her painting career and has since held many solo exhibitions in the UK and Auckland and exhibited in group shows mainly in Sussex, Hampshire and London.

George Bond
POUSSIN

George Bond is the interior designer best known for his breathtaking creations on ITV's *Better Homes* with Carol Vorderman.

Based in his hometown of Newcastle-upon-Tyne, Bond has his own design firm – Oma Designer Workshop Ltd - that creates stylish interiors for residential and commercial properties of all sizes, both in the UK and abroad. George's projects range from classical to commercial, modern to minima and he also creates bespoke furniture and designs for his clients.

Bond began designing in 1984, after training in London. Since then he has gained international recognition and has become a Member of Council and the Chairman of the Northern Region of the British Interior Design Association.

Bond's clients include Bianca Jagger, Jane Sartin, Carol Vorderman and Michael Owen and he regularly appears within the media as a style and design expert; his own home was recently featured in *25 Beautiful Homes* magazine and also *Beautiful Kitchens*.

Bond sources his inspiration from world travel and is currently producing designs f a collection of wallpapers and fabrics.

This is such an easy dish to do and makes the poussin really very tasty, if not the best ever. I have adapted the recipe from one of Jamie Oliver's books. A poussin is a very small chicken and most supermarkets now sell them. They look so small, and you might wonder if there is more bone than meat, but believe me, each one provides a substantial helping for each person.

Meal for 4

4 poussin
450g (1lb) potatoes, cut into wedges small enough to insert into the poussin cavity
handful of fresh herbs of your choice, I use rosemary (chopped)
olive oil (enough to coat potatoes)
garlic – be generous – about 10/12 cloves which I mince to bring out the full flavour
10–12 rashers of streaky bacon
glass of white wine

Preheat the oven high enough for roasting, say 220°C / 425°F / Gas mark 7.

Run cold water through each of the poussins, and cut away any pieces of fat, or flaps of skin, then pat dry. Meanwhile parboil the potatoes in salted water; remove from pan, pat dry, allow to cool.

Put wedges into a bowl with the minced garlic, chopped rosemary, salt and pepper and pour sufficient olive oil to coat – use your hands, even if messy, and ensure all the surfaces are coated. Insert as much of the potato as possible into each poussin cavity. Place the poussin on a roasting tray and surround with the remainder of the potato wedges, and cook for 30 minutes, at which time the poussin should look crisp and golden. Remove from oven and lay the bacon snugly over the breast meat and cook for a further 15 minutes.

Remove from oven and off the tray and allow to rest for five minutes, while you make a quick gravy. Remove as much fat as possible from the tray, and place tray on the hob with a gentle heat. Add a glass of dry white wine, simmering for two minutes, stirring gently and adding some cream.

At this point partially ease out some of the potato wedges from the cavity, to look more decorative, and serve with the other potato wedges and a nice fresh green vegetable – I like to use asparagus or spinach.

This is an easy recipe, particularly when you have a busy work schedule, and everyone loves it. Presentation is always important, and this looks great and certainly has the 'Wow' factor.

Baroness Virginia Bottomley
SWISS CHICKEN HAM BAKE

Serves 6

½ cup chopped onions
75g (3 oz) mushrooms, sliced
2 tablespoons butter or margarine
225g (8 oz) single cream
3 tablespoons plain flour
2 tablespoons dry sherry
½ teaspoon salt
2 cups cooked chicken or turkey
½ teaspoon pepper
1 cup cooked ham
1 can 150g (5 oz) water chestnuts drained and sliced
Soft breadcrumbs
3 tablespoons melted butter
4 oz shredded cheese

Cook onion in 2 tablespoons butter until tender but not brown. Blend in flour, salt and pepper, add mushrooms, cream and sherry. Cook and stir until thickened. Add chicken, ham and water chestnuts. Pour into casserole, top with cheese. Mix crumbs and melted butter and sprinkle round the edge of the casserole. Bake in a hot oven 200°C / 400°F / Gas Mark 6 until lightly brown, approximately 25 minutes.

The Rt Hon Baroness
(Virginia) Bottomley of Nettlestone was
Member of Parliament for South West Surrey
from 1984 until 2005. She was Secretary of State
for Health from 1992–1995 and Secretary of State for
National Heritage from 1995–97. She stood down at the
2005 election and was awarded a peerage the same
year. She is married to Peter Bottomley MP and has
one son and two daughters

Brookfield Hotel, Emsworth
MONKFISH IN FILO PASTRY

Serves 4

monkfish

600g monkfish tail, which has been skinned, boned and any membrane removed cut into four equal pieces
4 sheets filo pastry
4 slices Parma ham
24 large leaves basil (12 for deep-frying)
splash of olive oil (to seal monkfish with)
deep fat fryer for frying twelve of the basil leaves – this should be done quickly – approx thirty seconds then remove and drain reserve until needed
2 egg yolks beaten
2 lemons cut in half

salsa

1 large red onion finely sliced
6 large ripe plum tomatoes cut into quarters remove seeds cut into strips
100ml olive oil
good splash red wine vinegar
30g small capers or **larger ones roughly chopped**

Firstly heat up a frying pan. Add a splash of olive oil, season the monkfish lightly and seal quickly in pan. Remove and refrigerate for 10 minutes.

In a separate pot add the olive oil, red wine vinegar and red onion and place a lid on. Heat for approximately 5 minutes. Once it starts to bubble remove from heat and throw in tomatoes and capers, keep lid off and allow to infuse.

Take the monkfish out of the fridge, place your slices of Parma ham on the table. Place on to these 3 basil leaves and place on to that the monkfish width ways and roll it up.

Take your sheets of filo pastry.

Brush each sheet with beaten egg yolk. Place 1 piece of wrapped monkfish on to each sheet and roll up to make a neat parcel.

Panfry over moderate heat, turning occasionally for approx 10 to 15 minutes. Remove from heat, trim both ends then cut at a slant from one end to the other. Stand up on a warmed plate, spoon around salsa, garnish with a lemon half then add some of the deep fried basil leaves and serve. (Minted potatoes and green salad would be nice).

Tania Bryer
MALVA PUDDING

This is a South African dish. My father was South African and I grew up on it. We would always have it when we had family celebrations and went to visit relatives.

200g of self raising flour
175g brown sugar
2 eggs
50ml of apricot jam
100ml of melted butter
60ml honey

Pre heat the oven to 180°C / 350°F / Gas mark 4.

Whisk together the eggs and brown sugar.

Slowly stir in the flour with a metal spoon.

In a pan, melt the jam, butter and honey until just boiling. Remove from the heat and set aside.

Pour the flour mixture into a baking dish. Bake in the oven for 20 minutes.

Remove and pour syrup over the pudding.

Replace the pudding in the oven for an extra 20 minutes.

Remove and serve immediately with ice cream or fresh cream.

Tania is a professional presenter with a wealth of experience behind her. She has worked for all the major television networks specialising in the entertainment and showbusiness sector.

Pat Chapman
FRAGRANT BEEF SALAD with GRAPES
(Pla Nua Yaang Gub AA–Ngoon)

I learned this at chef's school in Bangkok. My instructor was at pains to advise that the grapes cost infinitely more than the steak. It is a gorgeous contrast of colour and tastes.

Strips of beef fillet marinated in minced coriander root, garlic and pepper, briskly stir-fried and tossed with herby leaves and black and white grapes, fragranced with finely chopped lemon grass, juliennes of fresh lime leaf, torn fresh harappa and holy Thai basil leaves, and juice of fresh kaffir (sweet lime).

250g lean fillet steak, weighed after stage 1
3 tablespoons sunflower or soy oil
1 tablespoon 'Magic Paste' (see facing page)
1 teaspoon palm sugar (or brown sugar)
2 lemon grass stalks, finely cut cross-ways
3 or 4 lime leaves, shredded
20 black and / or white seedless grapes, halved
squeeze of Kaffir lime juice
mixed salad leaves
fresh mint and basil leaves

1. Divest the steak of any unwanted matter. Cut it into thin strips, about 4cm x 2cm x 4mm each.

2. Heat the oil in your wok. Add the magic paste and stir-fry for 30 seconds. Add the meat strips, sugar, most of the lemon grass and 2 lime leaves, and briskly stir-fry for about 3 minutes, turning from time to time. You are trying to achieve a meat colour just browner than pink, for maximum tenderness.

3. Transfer the meat and liquid from the pan to a mixing bowl to stop the cooking.

4. When it is cold, add the grapes, and toss well.

5. On the serving plate, arrange the salad then place the beef onto it.

6. Garnish with the remaining lemon grass and lime leaf along with the mint leaves, and chilli tassle.

Tip: To cut thin strips of meat, chill the steak in the freezer for about 45 minutes. It is then hard but not frozen and it cuts easily.

Pat Chapman
MAGIC PASTE
(Lapakchee Prig Thai)

In many different parts of the world, you'll find a trinity of basic ingredients. In India it is garlic, ginger and onion, and in Cajun cooking the mixture of garlic, onion and peppers is called the 'Holy Trinity'. In Thailand the three ingredients are garlic, coriander leaves, stem and roots and white pepper corns (or fresh green pepper corns, if available). These are ground together to a paste and stir-fried in many a Thai dish. It is so important, that Thai call it their 'Magic Paste'.

Enough for many uses

5 cloves garlic
½ cupful fresh coriander, leaves, stems and roots
25 green or white pepper corns

1. Put the ingredients into the blender, and using just enough water, mulch it down to a purée. Alternatively, pound down to a coarse pulp in a mortar. Freeze excess paste.

'The Curry King' learned to cook the Pukka Indian way from his memsahib granny. He was educated at Bedales and Cambridge and had a short commission in the RAF flying fast jets. He later set up his own stage lighting and sound company. He was constantly asked by friends about spices and curry so in 1982 he founded *The Curry Club*. Today it has a huge following and he regularly appears as celebrity chef and takes culinary tours to India. Pat has made many guest appearances on TV and is contributing editor to *Tandoori* magazine. He has written many books on the subject his latest book is titled *The Real Fast Curry Cookbook*.

Pat Chapman
MOSLEM-STYLE CURRY WITH MUSHROOMS & PRAWNS
(Khaeng Mussaman Hed Gung)

The further south you go in Thailand, the closer you get to the Malaysian border, and the more Thai Moslems you'll find. Most people wear white Moslem dress and the mosques out number the Bhuddist temples by ten to one. At the town of Satun, for example, is a gold-domed mosque, near which are a number of roti khaeng (Indian flat bread with curry) stalls. One curry you'll be sure to get there is called Mussaman (Moslem being a tongue twister). This curry is the nearest in style to Indian you'll get in Thailand. Here is the typical Mussaman taste with oyster mushrooms and prawns.

Curry Paste (Lapakchee Prig Thai)

Makes enough for one Mussaman curry, but you can make more and freeze the surplus.

2 or 3 dry lime leaves (if available)
2 tablespoons sunflower or soy oil
6 to 8 cloves garlic
3cm cube ginger or galangal
2 tablespoons chopped shallot
1 tablespoon lemongrass, very finely crosscut
1 teaspoon fish sauce
1 teaspoon ground coriander
1 teaspoon turmeric
½ teaspoon ground cummin
½ teaspoon ground cardamom

1. Put the ingredients into the blender, and using just enough water, mulch it down to a purée. Alternatively, pound down to a coarse pulp in a mortar.

The Curry

Serves 4

24 raw King prawns, peeled but with tail on, each weighing about 22g to 25g
1 tablespoon dried prawns
150 ml of water or stock
½ teaspoon shrimp paste
4 to 6 oyster mushrooms
3 tablespoons sunflower or soy oil
1 batch Mussaman curry paste (see previous page)
200ml coconut milk
1 stalk lemongrass cut into a tassle
2 or 3 lime leaves
fish sauce or salt to taste

Spices

2 star aniseed
2 or 3 white (or green) cardamoms
5cm piece cassia bark
2 or 3 bay leaves

Garnish

some red chilli in strips or whole
some chopped fresh coriander leaves

1. De-vein and wash the King prawns.

2. Put the dried prawns into the stock and leave them to soak for an hour or so.

3. Quarter the mushrooms.

4. Heat the oil. Stir-fry spices for 30 seconds. Add the Mussaman curry paste and continue to stir fry for a further minute.

5. Add the soaked prawns, the coconut milk, lemongrass and lime leaves and bring to the simmer, stirring for a couple of minutes.

6. Add the King prawns and the mushrooms and simmer for about three more minutes. Salt to taste. Garnish and serve with Pad Thai and/or rice.

Pat Chapman
BANGKOK STREET NOODLES
(Pad Thai or Thai stir-fried noodles)

Of all the famous Thai dishes, Pad Thai (meaning stir-fry Thai) has to be the most prolific. It is the Thai national dish. You'll see it everywhere you go in Thailand, on every hotel and restaurant menu and on every street. And by far the best and cheapest is made by the pavement vendors, and you can see how they do it. It is easy to cook. It is a noodle dish to which almost anything can be added according to your taste. Here rice ribbon noodles are stir-fried with a sweet and sour sauce made from palm sugar and tamarind. Crab meat, prawns and freshly ground peanuts are added and all is fragranced with lemon grass tassels, lime leaf chiffonades, Thai basil, and a wee chilli kick!

Serves 4

Paste

4 cloves garlic
3cm cube galangal or ginger
1 teaspoon finely chopped lemon grass
1 teaspoon bottled red curry paste
½ teaspoon shrimp paste
½ teaspoon tamarind purée
1 or more red chillies, chopped
½ teaspoon palm sugar
2 tablespoons holy basil leaf
1 tablespoon coriander leaf

1. Put the ingredients into the blender, and using just enough water, mulch it down to a purée.

Alternatively, pound down to a coarse pulp in a mortar.

The dish

125g dried rice noodles
20 dried prawns (reconstituted in water)
3 tablespoons sunflower or soya oil
½ tablespoon chopped red bell peppers or red chilli
2 or 3 tablespoons bean sprouts
chinese vegetables such as pak choi, shredded
3 tablespoons chopped spring onions, leaves only
shreds of cooked chicken and pork (optional)
4 king prawns (optional)
2 tablespoons crab meat (mixed white & brown) [optional]
8 roasted whole peanuts, chopped
soy sauce and fish sauce to taste
egg (optional)

The method

1. Soak the noodles in cold water for one hour. This will soften them.

2. Soak the dried prawns in enough water to cover them.

3. During this, make the paste in a blender or by pounding in a mortar.

4. After the hour is up, heat the oil in the wok. Stir-fry the paste for 30 seconds.

5. Add the peppers, bean sprouts, Chinese vegetables and spring onion leaves, also the optional chicken and pork.

6. Add a little stock or water as needed but keep thing fairly thick in texture, and stir-fry for about 3 minutes.

7. Add the prawns and continue simmering for a further 3 minutes.

8. Strain the noodles and add them to the wok. Stir-fry for a couple of minutes during which time they fully soften, going translucent. Taste to test that they are as tender as you like.

9. Add the crab meat, the peanuts and the raw egg if wanted, quickly stirring it in so that it cooks onto the noodles.

10. Season with soy sauce and / or fish sauce.

Warning: Do not give this dish to anyone without checking whether they are allergic to peanuts.

Recipes from Pat Chapman's *Thai Restaurant Cookbook*

Sally Clarke
LAVENDER SHORTBREAD

Proprietor of the
famous *Clarke's* restaurant
in Kensington Church street, Sally Clarke
opened her restaurant in 1984 when it was
considered an innovation to have a set choice menu.
Sally Clarke's cooking has been influenced by her period
in California, cooking with Alice Walters at the iconic
restaurant *Chez Panisse*. Her bakery and shop produce
bread and ingredients for the restaurant and today
her bread has a large following across London
where it is sold in many top delis and
restaurants.

These unusual, fragrantly flavoured biscuits are a perfect accompaniment to many summer desserts, or just by themselves at teatime.

Sue Dicken

For 24 crescent-shaped biscuits

1 teaspoon finely chopped lavender blossoms (approximately 3 lavender heads)
100g caster sugar
200g unsalted butter
300g flour
pinch of salt

Mix the lavender with the sugar, then lightly cream it with the butter. Sieve the flour with the salt and mix together with the butter and sugar to make a soft dough. Chill for at least 1 hour.

Preheat the oven to 180°C / 325°F / Gas mark 3. Roll the dough out approximately 5mm thick and cut into crescents using a 8cm fluted cutter. Place on a baking sheet, sprinkle with a little castor sugar and bake for 15–20 minutes or until pale golden. They will become crisp on cooling. When cool store in an airtight container for up to 4 days.

Good luck with the appeal.

Sally Clarke

Jeremy Clarkson
BEANS à la CLARKSON

1 tin of Heinz Baked Beans (only Heinz – no imitations allowed)
lashings of butter
6 drops of Tabasco
good white bread

1. Find a can opener, open tin of Beans, put in a saucepan with two large knobs of butter and the Tabasco.

2. Heat the beans slowly over a low heat for a long time until the mixture becomes slightly mushy, the beans must still just resemble the shape of a bean but the mixture must be mushy.

3. Place two slices of bread in the toaster and toast lightly, butter the toast liberally making sure that the butter reaches every corner.

4. Place the beans all over the toast and serve immediately.

Jeremy Clarkson has presented BBC's *Top Gear* since 1989. He trained as a journalist and formed the Motoring Press Agency in 1984. As well as contributing to most specialist car magazines over the years – he was columnist for *Performance Car* from 1986 to 1993. In 1993, Jeremy presented *Clarkson's Star Cars* and then fronted two six-part series of *Jeremy Clarkson's Motorworld*. In January 1998 he presented *Jeremy Clarkson's Extreme Machines* and in 2000, *Clarkson's Car Years*. Jeremy has presented numerous other television programs and is the author of several books.

Melanie Clough
SPICED LENTIL SALSA

Melanie loved this recipe because it reminded her of the delicious lentil dish served at the Bel Air Restaurant on the slopes above Courcheval in France. She enjoyed many lunchtime ski breaks at this atmospheric restaurant, and the lentils, which always featured on the menu, were an excellent reason to stop by!

200g Puy lentils, soaked for 3-4 hours and washed
40g fresh root ginger, peeled and finely chopped
2 medium mild chillies, seeded and finely chopped
1 medium red onion, peeled and finely chopped
2 cloves garlic, peeled and crushed
1 teaspoon ground cumin
½ teaspoon cumin seeds
50 ml water
50 ml balsamic vinegar
50 ml sweet soy sauce or light soy
2 tablespoons tomato ketchup
1 tablespoon sweet chilli sauce
50 ml olive oil
15g fresh coriander, finely chopped
salt and pepper

Cook the lentils in salted water for 15–20 minutes or until they are tender. Drain and cool them. Place the ginger and chillies in a pan with the onion, garlic, ground cumin and seeds, water and balsamic vinegar and simmer with a lid on for a few minutes, stirring well so that all the flavours infuse. Remove the mixture from the heat and pour into a bowl with the drained lentils. Add the soy sauce, ketchup and chilli sauce, stir well and gradually add the olive oil and chopped coriander. Season, cover and leave in the refrigerator overnight (if time allows).

The Crown Hotel, Emsworth
EMSWORTH COCKLE & CRAB CHOWDER

Serves 4–6

10 oz local Emsworth cockles
6 medium size crab claws
8 oz potatoes cut into ½" cubes
1 large onion finely diced
1 oz clarified butter
3 oz salt pork or unsmoked bacon
10 fl oz milk (½ pint)
6 fl oz double cream
strained liquid from the cockles
1 bayleaf
pinch of cayenne
1 oz butter with 1 oz flour mixed to a thick paste (beurre manié)
salt & freshly ground pepper & a pinch of cayenne pepper
fresh chopped parsley to garnish

Thoroughly wash and clean the cockles, changing the water three or four times to ensure you clean out any grit. Ideally purge the cockles in salted water with a sprinkle of flour for about an hour.
Crack the cooked crab claws in a tea towel using a rolling pin keeping the pinchers intact for decoration. Put all the meat to one side.
Prepare the onions and potatoes, but do not wash as the starch will add body to the chowder.
Dice the pork into ¼ inch cubes or batons if preferred.
Thoroughly wash the parsley, squeeze dry in a clean tea towel and put to one side.

Steam cockles in a little water, as soon as they open remove from the heat and strain, saving the liquid.
Place potatoes in a saucepan, cover with milk and a little cream, add a bay leaf and simmer gently until potatoes are just cooked but still firm.
Fry the pork in the clarified butter until slightly brown, add chopped onion and sweat without browning. Add this to the potatoes with the liquid from the cockles and simmer for 3 to 4 minutes. Add a little salt, pepper and cayenne. If the chowder needs thickening add the beurre manié at this stage. Bring back to a gentle simmer and add the crab meat. Cook gently for one minute then add the cockles in their shells with the remaining cream and just heat through without cooking any further, as cockles tend to go tough if overcooked.
Pour into large bowls placing the pincher in the centre, garnish with chopped parsley.

Delicious with fresh crusty bread or croutons.

Phil Murphy (Chef)

Philippa Davenport
GUIDWIFE CHICKEN

I first made this soup-cum-stew one Sunday evening when friends turned up unannounced, and fridge and store cupboard were virtually bare but for the remains of a roast chicken we had had for lunch, a few basic vegetables, and herbs growing in pots on the kitchen windowsill. It fast became a firm favourite and I now always buy the largest bird I can in order to have leftovers to make Guidwife Chicken. (Guidwife is the Scottish name for a sensibly frugal housewife, by the way.)

There is something rewarding about making a good meal out of what are little more than leftovers, and I am deeply comforted and soothed by a simple meal-in-a-bowl like this that is effectively food and drink rolled into one. Two things make or break the pleasure of it for me. First, the company of those with whom it is shared. Second, the quality of the chicken. There is no point in trying to make a simple dish like this unless you choose a bird of good pedigree that has run free in life and been properly hung afterwards with white and brown meat that look and taste distinctly and deliciously different under a crisp skin and thin flavoursome layer of fat.

Quality of the chicken apart, this is a very flexible recipe. It is quick and unfussy to make, and easy to eat from soup or pasta bowls with spoons. Exact quantities are irrelevant. A bit more or less of this and that will do fine, and you should feel free to substitute. I have replaced the potato with parsnip or butternut squash on occasion, and used tarragon and parsley when no coriander is to hand. But here is my basic suggestion to serve 4 people:

As much meat as you can pick from the remains of **a large cold roast chicken**
leftover **chicken gravy**
about 1 litre chicken stock (the better the stock, the better the results. If you have no gravy, good home made stock is esssential and a slug of wine is recommended. If you have plenty of a good chicken gravy, you could make do with Marigold bouillon powder).
a walnut-size nugget of butter
3 leeks, 3 maincrop carrots and **3 floury potatoes**
a generous handful of fresh coriander
1 green chilli or a good pinch of dried chilli flakes (optional)
4–5 tablespoons mayonnaise (a good commercial brand will do) into which you have stirred
a large garlic clove creamed to a paste with **a little salt**

Peel the potatoes, scrape the carrots and trim the leeks, green parts as well as white. Chunk the potatoes quite small, cut the carrots and leeks obliquely into short lengths.

Scrape the fat from the top of the chicken gravy and melt it with the butter in a soup or stew pan. Add the prepared vegetables and stir and turn them for a minute or so to coat with fat. Pour on the gravy and stock (and wine if using it). Cover and simmer until the vegetables are half cooked.

Add the chicken meat (complete with skin), cut into chunks or picked from the bones, the chopped coriander and chilli. Cover again and continue simmering for about 7 minutes until the vegetables are done and the chicken is thoroughly heated through. Towards the end of this time, stir a small ladle of the hot chicken broth gradually into the cup of garlic mayonnaise.

When chicken and vegetables are ready, add the cup of garlic mayonnaise broth into the stew pan, stirring all the while. Check seasoning then let the covered pan stand away from the heat for 5 minutes before tucking in. Good bread, cheeses and fresh fruits to follow will round off things nicely.

Philippa Davenport worked for Christies fine art auctioners, in Sardinian property development, and in films (reading scripts and choosing locations) before she entered the world of food. She started writing for the *Financial Times* in 1973, when the newspaper first decided to carry food coverage. 32 years on, her award winning column remains one of the paper's best loved and most widely read Saturday features. Philippa has written five cookbooks, she devised and helped launch *Good Cooking*, the best selling cookery partwork of its day, and has contributed to various other newspapers and magazines over the years, including *Country Living*, for whom she was the regular cookery writer for 16 years, from the magazine's launch in 1985 until December 2001.

Sir Geoffrey Dear
GUINNESS CAKE

" – for those who like soggy fruit cake!"

225g (8oz) butter
225g (8oz) soft brown sugar
4 eggs – lightly beaten
275g (10oz) plain flour
2 level teaspoons of mixed spice
225g (8oz) seedless raisins
225g (8oz) sultanas
115g (4oz) mixed peel
115g (4oz) chopped walnuts
8–12 tablespoons of Guinness

Sir Geoffrey Dear was a serving police officer from 1956-97. All ranks in Service, in Cambridgeshire, Nottinghamshire (Assistant Chief Constable), Staff College. Metropolitan Police (Assistant Commissioner 1980–85), West Midlands (Chief Constable 1985–90), HM Inspector of Constabulary 1990–97. Awarded HM Queen's Commendation for Bravery 1979. QPM 1982. Knight Batchelor 1996. He is currently Deputy Lieutenant of Worcestershire.

Line a 7 inch cake tin with greaseproof paper.
Cream the butter and sugar.
Add the eggs.
Fold in flour and fruit, mixed spices and walnuts.

Add 4 tablespoons of Guinness, so that the mixture is a soft dropping consistency.

Turn into the lined cake tin and bake in a pre-set oven at 170°C / 325°F / Gas mark 3 for 1 hour, then at 150°C / 300°F / Gas mark 2 for a further 1½ hours.

Take out of oven and allow to cool.
When cool, prick the base and pour in the remaining Guinness.

Now for the crunch!

Wrap in foil and put to the back of the cupboard, out of temptation's way, for at least 2 weeks, during which time it matures, grows soggy and very special!

Anna del Conte
PASTA AL TONNO
(Pasta with Tuna Sauce)

In 2004 we spent a fortnight in Sicily in a friend's beautiful house. You looked North and there was the majestic Etna, gently (thank goodness) puffing away, while on the other side we were surrounded by lemon trees and in the far distance the most blue of all blue strips of sea. We went shopping in nearby Riposto, we went to have ice-creams and prosecco in Taormina, we lounged around the swimming pool and we cooked and cooked and cooked. We decided to have a competition as to who made the best pasta with tuna sauce, a classic Sicilian dish. So for about a week we had pasta with tuna every day, though certainly not every meal. Tuna sauce has the advantage that it can be prepared in a number of ways: with tomatoes or without, cooked or uncooked, with anchovies or without, pureed or in chunks, et al. Anyhow, this recipe, mine as a matter of fact, was the winner. A word of warning: buy only the best tuna, French or Italian, packed in olive oil.

Serves 4

2 or 3 garlic cloves, crushed
6 tablespoons extra virgin olive oil
1 diced chilli
a bunch of flat leaf parsley, chopped
2 salted anchovies, cleaned, rinsed and chopped, or **4 anchovy fillets,** drained and chopped
200g best canned tuna, drained
salt and freshly ground black pepper
350g Italian spaghetti
a dozen black olives, pitted

Put the garlic, oil, chilli and parsley in a large frying pan and sauté gently for a minute or two. Add the anchovies and tuna and cook for 10 minutes. Taste, add salt if necessary, and the pepper.

Cook the spaghetti according to the packet instructions. Drain when ready and turn it immediately into the frying pan. Stir fry for a couple of minutes, mixing constantly to coat the pasta with the sauce. Scatter the olives over the pasta and serve at once.

To quote Nigella Lawson – Anna is *'beyond doubt the best writer of Italian Food'*. Anna was born and brought up in Milan where she studied History at university. She has written many award-winning books; her latest is titled *Gastronomy of Italy*. She contributes to many magazines and journals worldwide.

Dame Judy Dench
BREAD & BUTTER PUDDING

275ml (10 fl oz) milk
70ml (1/8 pint) double cream
grated rind of half a small lemon
50g (2 oz) castor sugar
3 eggs
Pannetone cake
15g (½ oz) candied lemon or orange peel finely chopped
50g (2oz) currants
freshly grated nutmeg

Dame Judi Dench CH, DBE is
one of Britain's most respected stage,
film and TV actresses. In 1988 she was
made a Dame Commander of the Order of
the British Empire (DBE) and in 2005 a
Companion of Honour.

Heat oven to 180°C / 350°F / Gas mark 4

Butter a 2 pint (1 litre) oblong enamel baking dish.
Slice the Pannetone and butter it. Put one layer on the base of the dish, sprinkle with the candied peel and half the currants. Put another layer of Pannetone in the dish and sprinkle with the rest of the currants.

Put the milk and cream together in a measuring jug, stir in the lemon peel and sugar. Whisk the eggs in a small basin and add to the milk mixture. Pour the whole lot over the Pannetone and sprinkle with freshly grated nutmeg.

Bake in the oven for 30–40 minutes. Serve warm.

This is delicious and provides the perfect solution for what to do with those dry Italian cakes you get given at Christmas!

Fred Dinenage
FRED'S LAMB CURRY

1.15kg (2½ lbs) diced lamb e.g. shoulder or leg
2 tablespoons butter
2 tablespoons olive oil
2 spanish onions, chopped
2 garlic cloves, finely chopped
1 level tablespoon curry powder
¼ teaspoon ginger
¼ teaspoon turmeric
pinch of paprika
pinch of cayenne pepper
1 level tablespoon plain flour
salt and freshly ground black pepper
285ml (½ pint) natural yoghurt

Heat the butter and the olive oil in a thick-bottomed casserole dish. Add the chopped onions and garlic and sauté until the vegetables are transparent. Remove the vegetables to one side.

Add the meat to the casserole. Brown on all sides. Cook for a few minutes. Add the spices and flour. Return the vegetables. Stir in the yoghurt and season to taste. Simmer until tender – about 45 minutes to one hour.

Serve with a green salad and poppodoms. A bottle of French red wine rounds it off nicely!

Fred Dinenage is one of the South's longest-serving broadcasters. His television career began in 1964 with Southern Television. He is co-presenter of the award-winning *Meridian Tonight* and has also presented a number of other Meridian programmes, including *Southern Gold*, *Keep it in the Family*, *Annual Review of the Year* and *Under Offer*. He also presented a series of the political debate *Questions*, more than 100 editions of the networked panel game *Tell The Truth* and also 16 series of the children's programme *How 2*.

Fred Dinenage is also a Director of Portsmouth Football Club.

Ditcham Park School Cookery Club
SURPRISE CHICKEN in a PARCEL

'Surprise Chicken in a parcel' was the most requested recipe from the five course meal which the year 10 cookery club created. This meal was a fundraiser for the Khao Lak Community Appeal.

Serves 4

1 500g packet puff pastry
1 egg beaten with 1 teaspoon water
2 tablespoons olive oil
4 organic free range chicken breast fillets, boneless
4 ripe plums (or skinned peaches)
150g Yorkshire Blue cheese (or similar creamy cheese eg St Agur or Wensleydale)
8–12 slices air dried Italian Alpine ham, depending on size of chicken pieces (This ham is like Parma, but cheaper; use Parma for an even greater treat!)
6–8 shallots, finely chopped
freshly ground black pepper
2 knobs butter
2 tablespoons dry white wine

1. Beat the egg with the water for pastry glaze.

2. Cut the pastry into one third and two third pieces. Roll out the pieces, using a clean 10p coin to judge the thickness (the thinner the better).

3. Pull the skin off the chicken pieces, and wash carefully, pat dry with kitchen paper.

4. Cut through the edge of each chicken breast, nearly to the other side so that it opens out to two flattish pieces, joined in the middle. Put cling-film under and over each breast and hit it with a rolling pin to flatten it out a little. Season with pepper (no salt as there is enough in the cheese and ham).

5. Slice the cheese fairly thinly, halve the plums, take out the stones and cut into slices.

6. Put cheese and plum slices over one half of each breast. Fold over the other half of the breast to make a kind of sandwich.

7. Wrap each filled breast in 3 slices of ham, overlapping, quite tightly – but try not to rip the ham. (If you have difficulty, lay the over-lapping ham slices on cling film and use it to help you roll up a neat package).

8. Heat the oil in a frying pan until very hot. Fry the breasts in the oil, turning them until the ham turns golden and a bit crisp. (If you start frying with the loose ends downwards, this will help to seal the ham in place). Fry fairly fast, but for no more than about 4 minutes. Leave the fried pieces to cool.

9. While the chicken packages cool, chop the shallots, and sweat gently in a small saucepan to soften them. Don't let them brown. When soft, add the wine and let it evaporate, stirring occasionally. Stop while the shallots are still very moist, then add freshly ground black pepper. Keep aside.

10. Using the smaller piece of rolled pastry, cut rectangles for the base of each chicken parcel, leaving a 2cm border all round the chicken. Brush the borders with egg wash. Put some softened shallot on the top of each chicken piece.

11. Cut rectangles from the larger piece of pastry to fit over the chicken packages, with a 2cm border to fit the bases. Fit the tops as snugly as possible to the chicken pieces and press the borders together. Seal the pastry borders using the edge of the handle of a desert spoon, then trim the edges neatly. Cut a small hole in the top, then make leaves from the pastry trimmings, sticking them on with egg. Put the parcels on a baking sheet and glaze with egg wash.

12. Chill the parcels in the fridge for at least 20 minutes, to set the pastry. (The parcels could be made in the morning and cooked later if you are careful about cooling the chicken after frying).

13. When ready to cook, preheat the oven to 220°C / 425 °F / gas mark 7. Glaze the parcels again, bake for 20 minutes until golden brown, or 25 mins if the chicken fillets are large. Cover with foil if they are browning too much.

BON APPETIT!

We served these, as an alternative, with beef fillet, salmon or vegetarian parcels, at a five course formal evening dinner cooked by the cookery club. Accompaniments were pommes dauphinoise, haricot vert, small chantennay carrots and broccoli. If you are watching your weight, omit the pastry covering, and deglaze the pan after frying the chicken and ham with a little white wine, using this to heat the chopped shallots and gently fry the chicken for about 20 minutes. Delectable! Especially with rice.

David Fall (HM Ambassador to Thailand)
KHAO SOI

I am very happy to support this commendable project, and should like to propose a recipe for a simple northern Thai dish, Khao Soi. Its origins are far from the tsunami affected areas, but it is a dish I shall always associate with Thailand and the Thai people.

Curry Blend

1½ tablespoons red curry paste
15g galangal sliced
2 shallots
½ tablespoon turmeric powder

500ml coconut cream
500g chicken fillet, sliced
1 tablespoon palm sugar
1 tablespoon light soy sauce
1 chicken cube
400g egg noodles

David Fall has been HM British Ambassador to Thailand and Laos since August 2003, his third posting to Thailand.

In addition to Thailand, his overseas postings have been to South Africa, Australia (as Deputy High Commissioner) and Vietnam (as Ambassador). His areas of work overseas and in London have been in intelligence assessment, defence policy, personnel policy control, trade development and resource management.

Blend the curry mix first in a food processor. Then heat ½ cup of coconut cream in a wok. Add the curry mix and fry while stirring constantly for about 2 minutes. Add the chicken. Cook until almost done then pour in the rest of the coconut cream and bring to the boil.

Season with the palm sugar, chicken cube and soy sauce.

Cook the egg noodles in boiling water for 1 minute. Drain and keep warm.

Accompany with pickled cabbage, diced shallot, chopped spring onion, chilli flakes, lime wedge and crispy noodles.

"Staff of the British Embassy in Thailand, reinforced by family members, officers from other posts in the region, the British Police and Red Cross and by local British volunteers, were involved from the outset assisting British survivors of the tsunami and the relatives of the missing and in the complex and traumatic process of identifying the victims. They have chosen this simple, spicy recipe of a northern Thai dish, popular throughout the Kingdom, as a tribute to the outstanding assistance given by the Thai people and government to British and other people affected by the tsunami."

Fat Olives Restaurant, Emsworth
RED MULLET, TOMATO RISOTTO, BASIL OIL

For a starter serves four / main course serves two

4 small red mullet fillets (pin boned and scaled)

Basil Oil
1 bunch of Basil
25ml sunflower oil
25ml olive oil
pinch salt

Risotto
200g Arborio rice
1 medium onion, chopped
1 bay leaf
½ glass dry white wine
350ml fresh tomato juice (using an electric juicer)
seasoning
50g (2 oz) butter

Fat Olives is run by Lawrence & Julia Murphy in a small, 17th century fisherman's cottage in Emsworth, where modern English cuisine is influenced by the Mediterranean. Before setting up the Restaurant Lawrence & Julia travelled to some of the areas which are affected by the Tsumani. Like so many people who have encountered the warm hospitality of the Thai people they felt compelled to assist with this cookery book. Fat Olives is also hosting a cookery school where all proceeds will go to this great cause.

Make the Basil oil in advance by blanching the basil leaves in boiling water for ten seconds. Refresh them in iced water. Pat dry and place in a liquidiser with the oils and salt. Liquidise until puréed and strain through muslin. Put the oil into a small jug.

Place the tomato juice into a saucepan and warm slowly. Make the risotto by sweating the onion in a saucepan with 1oz of butter. Add the Arborio rice and fry until the rice is coated in the butter. Add the white wine and bay leaf. Gradually add the tomato juice, a ladle at a time, stirring the rice mixture continuously. Slowly the rice mixture will absorb the tomato juice. Do not over cook the rice – it should have a bite to it.

When the rice is nearly ready, pan fry the Red Mullet in olive oil skin side down first, then turn it over after about two minutes. Add the remaining butter to your risotto and check for seasoning. Spoon the risotto mixture into your serving dishes. Pour the Basil oil around the risotto and top with the Red Mullet.

Ursula Ferrigno
CAULIFLOWER from AMALFI

This is a wonderful way of preparing cauliflower. You will never enjoy cauliflower cheese in quite the same way again. My tip is to cook the cauliflower with some broken bay leaves to add a subtle bay flavour and also to take away the smell that cauliflower gives when cooking.

Serves 4

1 medium cauliflower
2 tablespoons white unbleached plain flour
2 free range eggs
4 tablespoons freshly grated Parmesan cheese
salt and pepper
3 tablespoons olive oil, for frying
flat leaved fresh parsley, to garnish

Break the cauliflower into florets then steam for 6 minutes until tender. Leave to cool.

Coat the cauliflower florets in flour, one at a time.

Beat the eggs then add the Parmesan cheese, salt and pepper. Dip the florets in the egg mixture.

Heat the oil in a frying pan and when hot, fry the cauliflower florets until golden and brown. Serve hot, cold or warm, scattered with parsley leaves.

Ursula Ferrigno is a talented vegetarian cook with a passion for southern Italian food. She is half Italian and learned to cook watching her grandmother preparing the traditional family dishes. She is a keen baker, featuring bread in many of her cookery demonstrations. She has appeared many times on television and has written numerous books such as *The Bread Book* and *Truly Madly Pasta*. Her latest cookbooks are *Trattoria* and *La Dolce Vita*.

Ursula Ferrigno
CHICKEN & ROASTED PEPPER SOUP
(Zuppa di pollo con peperoni arrostiti)

This recipe is based on a dish from the Ristorante Solferino in Tuscany, and it uses what they call "duchese" olive oil. This is made from olives grown on their own land and pressed locally. It is named after a family member, and is of very high quality. Use the best extra virgin you can get.

Serves 6

12 red peppers
10 chicken thighs
sea salt and freshly ground black pepper
2 tablespoons olive oil
1 onion, peeled and chopped
2 garlic cloves, peeled and crushed
1.5 litres (2½ pints) chicken broth
a handful of fresh basil leaves, torn
a handful of fresh mint leaves, roughly chopped
2 teaspoons marjoram leaves
duchese oil or the best-quality extra virgin olive oil

1. Preheat the oven to 200°C / 400°F / Gas mark 6. Roast the peppers for 25 minutes, then leave to cool. Scrape out the seeds and slice the peppers thinly.

2. At the same time cook the chicken thighs. Season them with salt and pepper and roast alongside the peppers for 20 minutes. Cool. Discard the chicken skin and bones and shred the meat finely.

3. Heat the oil in a large saucepan, add the onion and sauté until golden. Add the strips of peppers and the garlic.

4. Add the broth to the peppers along with the chicken shreds and herbs. Adjust the seasoning and simmer the soup for 5 minutes. Ladle into warmed soup bowls and serve with some good oil on top.

Ursula Ferrigno
APPLE & ROSEMARY CAKE

(Torta alle Mele e Rosmarino)

This is a quite delicious combination. I first enjoyed it in Venice and think the rosemary gives it a very memorable flavour. It is beautifully moist and is best eaten on the day it is made.

Serves 8–12

100g (4oz) unsalted butter
350g (12oz) Braeburn or Cox's Orange Pippin apples (about 3)
4 free range eggs
150g (5oz) caster sugar
150g (5oz) plain white or Italian type '00' flour
5ml (1 teaspoon) baking powder
pinch of salt
5ml (1 teaspoon) finely chopped fresh rosemary
finely grated zest of 1 unwaxed lemon
icing sugar, for dusting

Pre-heat the oven to 180°C / 350°F / Gas mark 4. Grease a 23cm (9 inch) deep round cake tin.

Melt the butter then set aside to cool. Core, peel and thinly slice the apples.

Put the eggs and sugar in a heatproof bowl, standing over a saucepan of gently simmering water. Whisk for 10–15 minutes until the mixture is thick, pale and leaves a trail when the beaters are lifted out. Remove the bowl from the heat and continue whisking until the mixture is cool.

Sift the flour, baking powder and salt together. Gently fold half the flour and the chopped rosemary into the whisked eggs and sugar.

Slowly trickle the melted butter around the edge of the bowl and gently fold in. (Take care not to stir the mixture too heavily or it will lose its air.)

Fold in the remaining flour and the lemon zest. Lastly, fold in the apples.

Pour the cake mixture into the prepared tin. Bake in the oven for about 40 minutes until a skewer, inserted in the centre, comes out clean.

Leave the cake to rest in the tin for about 5 minutes, and then turn out onto a wire rack and leave to cool.

Just before serving, sift icing sugar over the top of the cake.

Sir Ranulph Fiennes
MARS BAR CHOP

My favourite recipe is:

Chop a Mars bar (per person) into
smallish slices straight into a small
saucepan. Add 4 tablespoons of
milk (per person) and coffee granules
to taste (I use a teaspoon of coffee
for a serving sufficient for 4 people).
Use a wooden spoon to stir on a
hotplate until the chocolate has
become gooey. Add milk to achieve
the consistency you require.

*This goes extremely well with ice
cream!*

*Since my heart attack this now
has to be an infrequent, very
special treat.*

Sir Ranulph Fiennes Bt OBE is the world's
greatest living explorer. His expeditions
around the world include:

Transglobe: 1979/82 during which Ranulph
Fiennes and Charles Burton became the
first people ever to reach both poles by
surface travel.
North Polar Unsupported Expedition 1986
Anglo Soviet North Pole Expedition 1990/91
Co-leader of the Ubar Expedition 1991
Leader of the Pentland South Pole Expedition
1992/93

In 1993 he was awarded an OBE for 'human
endeavor and charitable service'.

Andrew "Freddie" Flintoff
FISH FINGERS, CHIPS & BEANS

Fish Fingers, Baked Beans and home made chips.

Fishfingers

Cook as directed on manufacturer's packaging.

Chips

Peel one large potato per person. Slice into chip size pieces.

Deep fry for 5/6 minutes.

Baked beans

Cook as directed on tin.

Andrew 'Freddie'
Flintoff is English and one of the best
all-round cricketers in the world. He plays county
cricket for Lancashire. He made his test match debut
for the England side in 1998 against South Africa. For his
achievements during the 2005 Ashes series, which was won by
England, he was named "Man of the Series" by Australian coach
John Buchanan. He also won the inaugural Compton-Miller
Medal. In October 2005 the Sir Garfield Sobers Trophy for
the ICC player of the year was jointly awarded to Andrew
Flintoff and Jacques Kallis of South Africa.

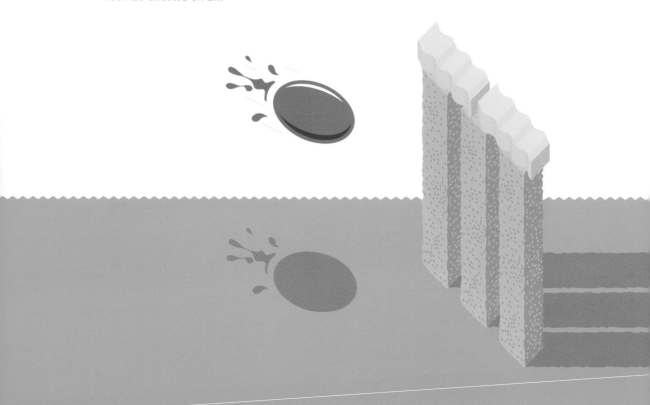

Moyra Fraser
PRAWN DISH

A very successful dish for the late night after-performance informal dinner.

500g – 600g small peeled prawns (well drained)
250g unsalted butter
black pepper
nutmeg
½ lemon

Deep serving dish such as a soufflé bowl

Melt the butter in a sauté pan.

Add the prawns to the pan and stir around until the prawns are cooked through.

Add the black pepper and nutmeg to taste.

Take a deep serving dish and place half a lemon in the bottom.

Pour in the prawn mixture and refrigerate.

Remove from the fridge 2 hours before serving.

Remove the lemon and serve with toast, a good white wine and some good company.

'About 45 yrs ago I was in a wonderful company at the Old Vic. Among them were Judi Dench, Maggie Smith, Joss Ackland, Alec McCowen and John Moffatt – we became firm friends. We try and meet for lunch occasionally – I made this prawn dish – they loved it – so I make it for them every time…'

Originally a ballet dancer with The Royal Ballet Company under Ninette de Valois, Moyra Fraser has spent most of her life acting – on stage, in film and on TV, starring in musical revue with the likes of Max Adrian and Joyce Grenfell, restoration comedy at The Old Vic with Judi Dench, Joss Ackland and Maggie Smith, playing Morgan LeFay in the musical *Camelot* with Laurence Harvey; in situation comedy such as *No Sex Please, we're British!* Moyra has also appeared in several films: *The VIPs, Left, Right and Centre, Here we go round the Mulberry Bush*; as Madame Dubonnet in Ken Russell's *The Boyfriend*. TV performances include: *The Good Life*, and most recently as Penny in the enduring favourite *As Time Goes By.*

Jane Fright
MUM'S OAT COOKIES

225g (8 oz) plain flour
225g (8 oz) caster sugar
225g (8 oz) porridge oats
225g (8 oz) margarine or butter
60g (2½ oz) golden syrup
2 teaspoons baking powder
2 teaspoons bicarbonate of soda
few drops vanilla essence

Jane co-owns the Oasis
Internet Café in Fuengirola, Spain with
her partner Jan. Much of the early work
on this book was carried out there and Jane
kept me sustained with the lovely cookies
she makes.

Cream together fat and sugar until light and fluffy. Add golden syrup and vanilla essence and beat for another 2–3 minutes.

Combine all dry ingredients and add to the mixture. Work together until a light dough is formed. Turn out onto a floured board and cut into 4 equal portions. With your hands, roll each portion into a long sausage shape, approx 12 inches. Cut into eight equal portions and roll each into a ball. Place on a greased and floured baking sheet. Lightly press flat with two fingers. Mixture should make approximately 32 cookies.

Cook for 30 minutes at 150°C / 300 °F / Gas mark 2

Susanna Gelmetti
LITTLE THAI CHICKEN RECIPE

Serves 4

8 chicken thighs, (1 kg) skinned
3 cloves of garlic, peeled and chopped
100g fresh ginger, peeled and chopped
1 fresh hot red chilli, finely chopped
1 small pot x 150g plain yoghurt
Juice of 1 fresh lemon

Place the chicken thighs in a terracotta oven dish.

Chop the garlic, ginger and red chilli to medium / fine dice and spread on the chicken

Add the yoghurt and lemon juice.

Make sure that all the pieces are covered and let it marinate for at least 20 minutes.

Place in a preheated oven at 220°C / 425°F / Gas mark 7 and cook, uncovered, for 40 minutes.

Born in Milan, Susanna was taught to cook by her maternal grandmother. She read modern languages in Milan before becoming a correspondent in London for *La Republica*. She launched her *Italian Cookery Weeks* catering courses and has a number of cookbooks to her name. She is the driving force behind the *Dress Italian* brand of food products, which are sold from her shop in Chelsea and selected supermarkets.

Serve with fresh tomatoes infused with basil and garlic and drizzled with extra virgin olive oil and black pepper.

Pippa Greenwood
VEGETARIAN PAELLA

2 **medium to large aubergines**
2 **red peppers**
2–4 **large cloves of garlic**
2 **medium red onions**
2–3 **small courgettes**
1 **can organic kidney beans,** rinsed
2–3 **fresh bayleaves**
250g **button mushrooms**
10 **medium to large tomatoes,** skinned
1 **lemon,** juiced
250g **brown rice**
180g **toasted flaked almonds**
extra virgin olive oil
salt and pepper

This is a great dish often enjoyed by otherwise rampant meat-eaters! Great to use organic ingredients if possible, and if you grow your own vegetables then you can obviously alter the ingredients slightly to make best use of any seasonal cropping-gluts!

Cook rice until tender and whilst it's cooking: Chop garlic and onions, plus bay leaves, and sauté until just transparent in oil. Then add diced aubergines, peppers (seeds removed and flesh cut in to strips). Cook for a few minutes and then add mushrooms and courgettes and the drained kidney beans. Cook for a few more minutes, stirring occasionally. Grind some pepper (to taste) over the mixture, then add lemon juice plus a little more pepper and some salt, to taste. Next add the rinsed, cooked rice and heat through. Whilst it's heating add the tomatoes (cut in to 4–6 pieces depending on their size) and the toasted almond flakes.

Pippa is one of the UK's leading plant pathologists. She ran the Royal Horticultural Society's plant pathology department in Wisley for 11 years and now lectures on gardening throughout the world. She has written numerous gardening books and is a regular panelist on BBC *Gardeners' Question Time.* She is a passionate vegetarian.

Grab some large bowls, some good friends and a bottle or two of your favourite tipple, turn off the 'phone and eat and chat to your heart's content.

Richard Griffiths
FABADA

Richard counts Fabada, the classic Spanish dish of beans among his favourite dishes.

Serves 6

250g (9 oz) tomatoes peeled and deseeded
900g (2 lb) rump steak
350g (12 oz) onions, chopped
3 celery sticks, chopped
2 courgettes, sliced
2 teaspoons sunflower oil
570ml (1 pint) beef stock
570ml (1 pint) tomato pasta sauce
425g (15 oz) can of haricot beans, drained
200g (7 oz) sweetcorn
2 tablespoons chopped fresh oregano
Seasoning to taste

Richard Griffiths comes from Cleveland in the north of England, and has been playing a rich and colourful variety of roles on stage, film and television for more than 30 years. He is familiar as Harry Potter's monstrous Uncle Vernon in the smash hit film series, delighted his fans as the detective turned chef in the series *Pie in the Sky*, is the voice of Jeltz in *The Hitchhiker's Guide to the Galaxy* and is to be seen in *Bleak House* and *The History Boys*.

Peel, deseed and chop the tomatoes.

Trim any fat from steak, and cut into small pieces.

Peel and chop the onions, slice celery, and cut the courgettes into thin sticks.

Heat the oil in a large pan and when it is really hot, fry the steak to seal and brown it and remove to a covered dish.

Cook the onions over a lower heat until softened and add the celery and cook for one minute.

Add the stock, pasta sauce, tomatoes, courgettes and beef.

Finally stir in the drained haricot beans together with the sweetcorn. just before serving add the chopped, fresh oregano.

Bryan Hamilton
VIETNAMESE SALAD

Serves 6

salad

500g sliced cooked chicken
500g of shredded white cabbage
150g of carrot (julienne strips)
6 spring onions sliced
3 tablespoons coarsely chopped mint leaves
3 tablespoons coarsely chopped coriander leaves

dressing

3 tablespoons of fresh lime juice
3 tablespoons of oriental fish sauce
1 tablespoon white wine vinegar
3 cloves of crushed garlic
2 tablespoons of sugar
3 tablespoons of vegetable oil (not olive oil)
*****2 chillies,** seeded and finely chopped

*I use a jar of minced chillies and add to taste

Prepare salad ingredients in large bowl, mix well.
Prepare dressing, pour over salad and mix well.

Enjoy

Bryan Hamilton
Ipswich, Everton, Manager of Northern Ireland

Following a great
playing career with Ipswich Town,
during their most successful period under
Bobby Robson, and Everton, as well as playing for
and captaining his country – Northern Ireland, Bryan
was manager at Tranmere Rovers, Wigan, Leicester
City, Norwich City and Northern Ireland. He is
now a very popular commentator for BBC 5
Live, Eurosport and for various radio and
TV channels.

Susan Hampshire
A SLIMMER'S LUNCH

2 heads broccoli
shredded ginger
olive oil
Fiddes Payne herb salt
1 tomato
squeeze of lemon

Take 2 heads of broccoli and steam. Add shredded ginger, then drizzle olive oil and sprinkle with herb salt. To finish add a steamed or fresh cut tomato and a squeeze of lemon.

If you want to be even healthier add 15 almonds or a tin of sardines.

Drink a glass of water before you eat.

A well respected and much loved actress of both the stage and screen. She won Emmy awards for her role as the determined Fleur in *The Forsyte Saga*, for the ambitious Becky Sharp in *Vanity Fair*, for Sarah in *The First Churchills* and then as Glencora in *The Pallisers*. We know her most recently as Molly in *Monarch of the Glen*. Susan Hampshire wrote a memoir, *Susan's Story* (1981), telling of her struggles with dyslexia and she received an OBE in 1995 for her work in this field.

SUSAN HAMPSHIRE

Sarah Jefferies
The Khao Lak Community Appeal

Dear Sarah Jefferies

Thank you for your letter and request for a recipe for the book, I enclose one of my favourite 'slimming' recipes. Wishing you every success with the Recipe Book.

All best wishes

Jo Hansford
PRAWN & ASPARAGUS RISOTTO

Serves 6

400g Arborio rice
1 tablespoon olive oil
2 shallots
2 cloves of garlic
50g (2 oz) butter
100ml white wine
2 pints Bouillon vegetable
stock
75g (3 oz) Parmesan cheese
500g pre-cooked and peeled prawns
200g asparagus tips

Jo Hansford, once dubbed 'the best tinter on the planet' by *American Vogue*, is without doubt the UK's leading authority on hair colour. Her specialist colour salon, in the heart of Mayfair, is hairdressing home to many celebrity heads, and houses an unrivalled team of the best hair colourists and stylists in London today.

Heat oil and add chopped shallots and garlic. Sauté for 5 minutes until the shallots are soft.

Add the rice and on a medium heat stir for 5 minutes and then add the wine to rice.

Heat the stock in a separate pan until boiling and start adding to rice, keeping on a medium heat and stirring continuously.

Make sure that the rice has absorbed the liquid before adding more.

When all the stock has been added and rice is cooked 'al dente', approximately 15 minutes, add the cooked prawns & asparagus tips and cook for a further 5 minutes, and then add butter and Parmesan.

Serve and eat as soon as possible.

Alastair Hendy
WOK FRIED BASIL
& CHILLI CHICKEN

A Bangkok easy. You can't go wrong. Very tasty.

4 small skinned chicken breasts, chopped
3cm fresh ginger
4 hot red chillies, deseeded and roughly chopped
4 fat cloves garlic
4 coriander roots, scrubbed (optional)
3 tablespoons oil – vegetable, peanut
2 tablespoons palm sugar
2 tablespoons Thai fish sauce
3 mild red chillies, deseeded and thickly shredded
big handful Thai basil leaves
(You will also need a large flameproof casserole dish or a wok)

Briefly pulse the chicken breasts in a processor until course-minced but not mushed. Pound the ginger, chillies, garlic and roots (if using) with a touch of salt to make a paste, then stir-fry in the oil in a wok for about a minute – until it looks golden. Tip in the chicken and toss through and stir-fry until it browns, then stir in the sugar and fry until things look sticky. Toss through the fish sauce and mild chillies and stir-fry for a further minute or so. Shift from the heat and toss through the basil, and serve. Something to scoop up with is in order – crisp salad or trimmed tender cabbage leaves.

A brilliant cook and entirely self taught, Alastair studied theatre and costume design at Central St Martins followed by a stint as display manager for Habitat. His career took off when he was runner up in the BBC Good Food Magazine Italian Cook of the Year. Alastair is a regular contributor to the Mail on Sunday and was *The Sunday Times* food and cookery writer. He contributes to many magazines such as *BBC Good Food, Olive* and *Sainsbury's Magazine, Food and Travel, Australia's Vogue Entertaining* and *Travel* magazine where both his travel writing and photography are featured. He won the best food journalist and best food photographer at the 2003 and 2005 World Food Media Awards. Alastair is constantly travelling and you can see the influence of his travels in his cooking.

'It's hot, it's steamy. And, it's exhaustingly busy. Chatujak, Bangkok's biggest market, has opened its gates to yet another frantic weekend of buy, sell and scoff – to hearts content. Bowls of this and woks of that, fly, dip, flip and duck.

Wide-line noodles and deep pans of steaming stock glint. Lipstick flashes of chopped phrik spin from boards into bowls, and the salt of naam pla steeps the shadows. Saucing, dipping, and spooning, shoppers eat – satiating tongues and convalescing swollen feet. I park-up too and sweat over a bowl of soup noodle, bobbing with fish ball. Phew, it's hot, but deliciously so.

Chatujak's core is a sauna of teenagers, denim, Gucci fake and flimsy T shirt club gear, while its outerlayers selling homewares, from the urban tasteful – palmwood bowl minimalism, to 2-baht kitchen plastic. At its perimeter, the bowl-food stalls full-steam it, under a venting rag-tag of canopies. Its vast maze of alleys would take days to cover, yet meltdown for me is near, and I beat a trail from its throbbing caldera, carried by the lava of cram, sweat and jostle, and am propelled out, ejected into flower-scented daylight.'

from **Food and Travels: Asia** by Alastair Hendy, published by Mitchell Beazley.

Lady Isabella Hervey
ISABELLA 'MASTERCHEF' CHICKPEA PASTA

Serves 2

250g broccoli
5 teaspoons green pesto
1 jar of grilled artichokes in olive oil
1 garlic clove
1 packet of chickpea pasta
Parmesan cheese
extra virgin olive oil
salt and pepper

Lady Isabella Hervey
is the daughter of the 6th Marquess
of Bristol. She is probably most well known
for receiving a gold medal on the Channel 4
reality TV show *The Games* (2004) and for appearing
as a contestant on ITV's *Celebrity Love Island*
(2005). Renowned for her amazing bikini body,
Lady Isabella is releasing her first fitness DVD,
Isabella's Power Workout in December
2005.

In one saucepan boil the pasta according to the pack instructions.
Boil the broccoli for approximately 6 minutes, in a separate saucepan.
Heat a teaspoon of extra virgin olive oil in a non-stick frying pan.
Chop the garlic finely and fry until golden brown.
Add pesto and artichokes to the garlic and mix in with the chickpea pasta.
Grate as much Parmesan on top as desired.
Season with salt and pepper to one's own taste.

Serve with a green side salad with balsamic vinegar.

I love experimenting in the kitchen with loads of my favourite foods - one of which is pasta. I made this one up a couple of years ago when I was training for the first television series of 'The Games'. Apart from the fact that all of the ingredients are delicious, they are also highly nutritious and very good for your general well-being. Broccoli is one of the best antioxidants and is full of vitamins. Chickpeas are protein based as well as carbohydrates, this, mixed with pasta, are ideal while in training - as you need the protein to build muscle and you need the carbohydrate as a slow energy release. Artichokes are very good for your veins and arteries, and they also act as a diuretic for water-retention. Garlic is great for your hair, nails and general well-being. It is important that you always use olive oil rather than other cooking oils, such as sunflower or vegetable, as olive oil has all the essential omega fatty acids that you need to keep your joints supple and your bones strong.

Lucy Elizabeth Holland
THAI CHICKEN CURRY

100g butter
1 can of coconut milk
400g sweet corn
1 pint of Tom Ka paste
8–10 leeks
6 chicken thigh portions (or breast depending on preference)
Basmati rice

Melt the butter in a large casserole dish and add chicken. Cook through until the inside is no longer pink. Trim and chop the leeks into chunks. Then add the pint of Tom Ka, sweetcorn in its juice, coconut milk and leeks. The liquid should cover the vegetables and chicken, you may need to add some water to it at this point. Bring to the boil. Heat the oven to 180°C / 350°F / Gas mark 4. Once the dish has simmered for 2–3 minutes cook slowly in the oven for 60–90 minutes. Serve on top of Basmati rice. It will feed 4 to 6 people.

This was Lucy's Sunday exeat comfort food. It wasn't really a curry or even very Thai, but it became known as that. Lucy's alternative to Sunday roasts; it always reminded her of home! Definitely one to pig out on!

Jane Mary Holland (née Attenborough)
PEACHES & PEARS IN WINE

14 firm peaches
4 firm pears
600 ml of red wine
2 cinnamon stick
2 vanilla pods
100g of caster sugar
1 lemon
crème fresh or ice cream

Pre heat the oven to 200°C / 400°F / Gas mark 6 and grease a baking tray large enough to hold the fruit when halved. Add the juice of one lemon, the wine and caster sugar, cinnamon and vanilla to a frying/ large saucepan. Bring the mixture to the boil and then reduce to a simmer. Peel, half and core the peaches and pears. Add the fruit to the mixture for 10 minutes, basting regularly. Then place the fruit on the baking tray hollow side up and bake on the middle tray for 4-6 minutes or until browned. Meanwhile boil the sauce up into syrup and decant into a jug. Then remove vanilla and cinnamon. Finally place fruit flat in a dish, spoon syrup over and cover with foil, leave to sit and refrigerate for 24 hours before serving. Lastly spoon the syrup over the fruit before serving with Crème fresh or Ice cream.

This was an amalgamation of various recipes adapted to what was in the fridge, as was the basis of all my Mum's cooking. One of Mum's dinner party favourites. Reassuringly indulgent and alcoholic! This is a dessert she felt could only be legitimised by sharing it with others!

(Audrey) Jane Holland
CHICKEN CASSEROLE

8 chicken thighs
butter for cooking
250g carrots
1 onion
2 leeks
250g button mushrooms
150g potatoes
150g swede
garlic
2 tablespoons of flour
500ml of chicken stock

Prepare leeks, carrots, potatoes, swede by leaving the skins on and cutting into inch sections. Dice the onion, crush the clove of garlic and wash the mushrooms leaving them whole. Cook the chicken through in butter in a large casserole dish with the onions. Remove the chicken to one side. Then add the flour, all the vegetables and a little of the stock, stir to a smooth consistency. Slowly add the rest of the stock and continue to stir. Add the chicken and bring to the boil. Then put the casserole in a well-heated oven 180°C / 350°F / Gas mark 4 and cook for 1 hour and 15 minutes, until the vegetables are cooked through. The dish is best if left to stand for 24–48 hours before serving.

This was one of my Grandmother's staples, epitomising home cooking. She had cooked since my Dad was a child! If she'd been house sitting, they'd always be one left in the fridge for us with a fish pie!

Eamonn Holmes
CHAMP

This is a delicious Irish speciality which is simple and quick to cook. It should be served with plenty of melted butter drizzling down – but the health conscious can reduce this.

Serves 4

900g (2lb) floury potatoes
spring onions
25g (1oz) butter
4 tablespoons milk
salt and freshly ground black pepper
knobs of butter to serve

In separate pans, boil the potatoes and onions in lightly salted boiling water until tender (the onions will cook for a much shorter time than the potatoes).

Drain both and mash the potatoes in a bowl with the butter and the milk.

Add the onions to the potatoes and mix in with some seasoning.

Heap into a bowl and make a hollow in the centre of the mash.

Add extra knobs of butter and serve immediately.

Belfast-born Eamonn Holmes trained as a journalist with Ulster Television, he took over from Gloria Hunniford as host of *Good Evening Ulster* at the age of only 21.

In 1993 he successfully took up residence on the GMTV sofa as co-presenter.

Game shows he has presented include: *Jet Set, Jet Set Departure Lounge, Hard Spell, Pass the Buck, Playing for Time, Pot Black Timeframe* and *Remotely Funny*. Other shows have included *How do they do that?, The National Lottery Live* and *Sporting Greats*. He also presents a weekend show on Radio Five Live.

Eamonn has recently become co-presenter of SKY early morning news programme *Sunrise*.

He is a huge Manchester United Fan!

Jane Horrocks
CHICKEN & MANGO SALAD

Serves 6

1 cooked chicken taken off the bone (organic is nicer)
4 tablespoons mango chutney
2 teaspoons crushed garlic
root ginger (a thumb-sized piece)
1 tablespoon light soya sauce
1 tablespoon lemon juice
1 tablespoon brown sugar
1 bag mixed salad leaves
1 sliced mango
6–8 tablespoons French dressing
cashew nuts (optional)

Heat chutney, garlic, ginger, soya sauce, lemon juice and sugar until mixed together. Cool. Add flaked chicken. Mix with salad leaves and mango. Sprinkle on nuts and add the dressing.

Jane Horrocks is a successful character actress of the stage and screen. She trained at RADA and then joined the Royal Shakespeare Company. She is probably best known for playing the part of Bubbles in *Absolutely Fabulous*. She played the troublesome teenager in *Life is Sweet* (1990) and was the singing heroine in *The Rise and Fall of Little Voice*, which was written for her. She is also well known for the series of Tesco ads.

Mark James
MARK'S CAJUN PORK

My wife and I tend to enjoy 'guessipies', rather than recipes. Mainly because we are usually cooking somewhere in the world without a recipe book for reference. This is one of our favourites, which is a variation on a Cajun Jambalaya dish. We were recently in Long Island, New York, where I was competing in a 'Champion's Tour' golf tournament, and unable to find chicken breasts less than the size of a small bus, so substituted with pork fillet. This basic recipe is a favourite of ours, because it can be prepared on just one hotplate, no oven required, which is often our only option.

2 (ish) tablespoons olive oil
few slices of chorizo (or other spicy sausage)
450g ish (1lb) pork fillet
salt and freshly ground black pepper
1 large onion, chopped
few sticks celery, chopped
1 or 2 green peppers, chopped
plenty of garlic, chopped (keeps marshalls at bay!)
approx ¾ pint chicken stock
cayenne pepper
1 bouquet garni (v. optional)
about 1 cup long grain rice

Heat the oil in a large pan and add the sausage. Cut the pork into thick slices, season and add to the sausage in the pan. Fry the meat until browned, then add the onion, celery, green pepper and garlic. Cover with the stock, add the bouquet garni, salt and as much cayenne pepper as you can stand, (we like it fairly hot). Place a lid on the pan and simmer for about ten minutes. Turn the heat right down until it's barely hot. Add the rice.
Leave for approximately twenty minutes until the rice is cooked. Keep an eye to make sure it doesn't go dry; if necessary, add a bit more stock.

Enjoy!!

Mark James is an English golfer who had a long career on the PGA European Tour and captained Europe in the 1999 Ryder Cup. He now successfully plays senior golf on the Champions Tour, and in 2004 became the first European player to win one of the Champions Tour's senior majors at the Ford Senior Players Championship. He then won the ACE Group Classic in 2005.

Mark James has penned two books *Into the Bear Pit* (2000) and *After the Bear Pit* (2002).

Charles Jardine
CEEJAY'S HOT ROASTED SALMON & PASTA

Charles Jardine is the pre-eminent fisherman of his generation. Writing, painting, illustration, public speaking, TV and radio and fly tying are just a few of his skills. He is Britain's most famous and internationally renowned fisherman.

I love the simplicity and ease of this dish. I strongly suggest that you serve it in a vast bowl, with wads (that's a chunk) of warm bread – anything nutty and brown: walnut is especially good. I also urge that you serve it whilst sitting by a river, having just fished. If you really must, then your dining table will have to do. If you crave authenticity in the home, get someone to make gurgling noises like running water, and eat whilst wearing waders. Well, it's a thought. A bad one perhaps … Anyway…

1 Boil a really big pan of water add some salt and a dollop or two of olive oil to help glaze and "loosen" the pasta (on the water amounts, add to the advised amounts indicated on the chosen pasta packets).

2 Place in the pan of boiling water the pasta sufficient for your needs. I tend to add a fistful per person – it is a very imprecise way of doing things. My hands are big and people have big portions. You can use almost any type of pasta but my preference is for Linguini or Tagliatelle as it seems to hold the flavour well. I quite like the organic variety – or you could make your own if you are good at cat's cradles. Actually, this dish suits most pasta types but the "ribbon" types seem to be best.

3 Cook the pasta so it is 'al dente', then drain and return the empty pan to the heat and quickly add some more olive oil – good stuff – two good slugs with your thumb over the bottle's opening should do it, to the drained pasta and then crumble some hot roast smoked trout or salmon (hot roast smoked salmon or kiln cured is really a cross between hot and cold smoking and produces wonderfully flakey and mild smokey flavours.) Two tablespoons of smoked fish flakes per person should do it. Add then a (minimum) dessertspoon of small capers per person, a tablespoon of chopped sun dried tomatoes, a good amount of coarse fresh ground black pepper. And a squeeze of half a cooked lemon (nope I haven't gone mad.)

4 Take a lemon, cut it in half then pan fry it – sear it really. Allow it to cool, then squeeze half of it into the pasta. Cooked lemon changes dramatically in flavour and becomes a "warmer" flavour and less tart.

5 Stir, over a moderate heat, sufficient to heat the dish through very quickly and not too much so that the pasta sticks to the pan bottom. If you over stir you will destroy the fish flakes – try and keep these whole and chunky. Once heated through and just as you are about to tip the whole thing into the serving bowl toss in a handful of roughly chopped flat parsley – or torn Basil for a stronger flavour – per person and a dessertspoon of venerable Balsamic vinegar – the old antique stuff that drinks almost like a sherry.

6 Eat the whole thing with a simple green salad tossed in a very unfussy oil and vinegar dressing.

7 Having enjoyed, go fish and work it off prior to pudding: well, it's a plan.

I hope you enjoy this recipe and it is a jolly good excuse to start to fish so that you catch your own trout that will ultimately grace this dish in the future. Good fishing and merry eating.

Sir David Jason
ROASTED TOMATO & GOATS' CHEESE TART with THYME

Courtesy of good old Delia...
This is a really good, easy way to use up a glut of
home grown tomatoes and is best served with a lightly
tossed salad. A real summer dish.....

Serves 6

I guarantee, once you've made this tart, you will go on making it because it's just about the easiest and most sublime tomato recipe on record. It's great as a starter or as a main course with salad. Serve it at barbeques or any outdoor eating event (it's even good cold on a picnic). You'll just have to make it to believe it.

1 lb 10 oz (740g) ripe plum tomatoes
5 oz (150g) soft goats' cheese
4 teaspoons fresh chopped thyme, plus a few small sprigs
1 x 375g pack fresh ready-rolled puff pastry
2 cloves garlic, peeled and crushed
2 tablespoons extra virgin olive oil
salt and freshly milled black pepper

You will also need a large baking tray 12 x 16 inches (30 x 40cm), lightly oiled.

Pre-heat the oven to gas mark 5, 375°F (190°C).

Most highly regarded British actor, admired equally for his dramatic work as for his comedy roles. In 1993 he was made an Officer of the Order of the British Empire (OBE), and in the Queen's Birthday Honours list of 2005 he was knighted for services to acting.

To begin the recipe, first of all unwrap the pastry and then place it on the baking sheet. Then, using a sharp knife, carefully score a line on the pastry about ½ inch (1cm) in from the edge, all the way round but be careful not to cut all the way through.

Now tip the goats' cheese into a small bowl, add the crushed garlic, chopped thyme and a good seasoning of salt and freshly milled black pepper. Then give it a good mixing, and using a small palette or other round-bladed knife, carefully spread the cheese mixture evenly all over the surface of the pastry, right up to the line.

Next, thinly slice all the tomatoes (there is no need to peel them) and arrange them on top of the goats' cheese in overlapping lines lengthways; overlap one line one way and the other next to it the other way. After that, season the tomatoes and then drizzle the olive oil and scatter the sprigs of thyme all over them.

Bake in the pre-heated oven on a middle shelf for 55 minutes or until the pastry is golden brown and the tomatoes are roasted and slightly charred at the edges. If you are going to serve the tart warm, leave to settle for about 10 minutes before cutting into squares.

Jay (Jamiroquai) Kay
GRIDDLED CHICKEN PASTA
with SPINACH & PARMESAN

Serves 4

4 x 200g skinless chicken breasts
500g dried pasta (tortellini)
2 fresh chillies, chopped
2 cloves garlic, chopped finely
1 x 20g pkt parsley
½ (150g approx) packet of baby spinach
parmesan cheese
dried oregano
salt
ground black pepper
olive oil

Cooking time: 30 minutes

Jamiroquai

Heat a large frying pan with olive oil. Throw garlic and chilli into hot oil and fry until slightly golden. Take off the heat and add the parsley. Heat a large pan of salted water and while waiting, season the chicken with the salt, pepper and oregano. Place chicken on a hot griddle and cook until well done. Boil the pasta in salted water and throw spinach in for the last half minute. Drain contents thoroughly in colander and place back into the pan. Add the contents of frying pan, mix well and place on plates. Slice the chicken and place on the top of the pasta. Add a generous amount of grated Parmesan on top.

Enjoy – great comfort food!!

A British musician, Jay is the main composer and lead singer of *Jamiroquai*, who have sold over 20 million albums and made 4 world tours in the 13 years since their creation. Jay Kay is also well known for his love of fast cars.

Normandie Keith
APPLE CRUMBLE

Born and raised in Manhattan, Normandie Keith has always had a love of fashion. Discovered by IMG, Normandie initially worked as a model in commercial and print, and travelled extensively. When she was twenty she moved to London and signed immediately with Models One, and never looked back – being shot for magazines such as *Tatler, Vogue, Harpers & Queen*. Her presence on London's social scene made her a name that is synonymous with both style and fashion, and introduced her to her husband, The Hon Lucas White.

Working as a model fed Normandie's insatiable hunger and good eye for new trends and gave her first hand experience of the beauty industry – Normandie's true passion! This led to Normandie's appointment as Beauty Editor at Large for *YOU* magazine, where she writes a weekly column for the publication and now the opportunity to create her own body care range – *Normandie*.

My favourite dish is apple crumble which I absolutely demolish the top off leaving the healthy apples for others. I am just a crumble kinda girl.

Serves 8

4 cooking apples
240g (8 oz) self-raising flour
55g (2 oz) granulated sugar and 2 tablespoons - on the apples
55g (2 oz) demerara sugar (brown, tough sugar) and 2 tablespoons on the crumble
110g (4 oz) butter

Peel all the apples and slice them. Set aside.

In a bowl, add granulated sugar, demerara sugar and flour. Then add the butter – and using your hands, rub it in. Continue this until the mixture is lumpy – but do not make it too firm.

Place the apples in a dish suitable for cooking in the oven, and place the crumble on top of the apples. Sprinkle the demerara sugar on top.

Bake in a pre-heated oven at about 180°C / 350°F / Gas mark 4.

Remove from the oven after 30–40 minutes or when brown.

And voila! It is delicious served with custard, cream or ice-cream or all of the above!

Lorraine Kelly
THAI GREEN CURRY PASTE

The green of this curry paste comes from the fresh coriander leaves. Like all plant materials, the natural chlorophyll (green colour) oxidises in air, fading rapidly on picking and cooking. Although this paste will last for up to a week in the refrigerator, it should be used within 2 days for maximum impact, colour and flavour. It is best for the clear, hot, sour/sweet curries much beloved of the Thais.

15 green chillies, chopped
4 spring onions or 1 large onion, peeled and chopped
3 cloves garlic, peeled and roughly chopped
1 tablespoon oil
1 tablespoon chopped galangal or ginger
2 tablespoons fish sauce
1 tablespoon sugar
1 teaspoon blachan (shrimp paste) or 2 teaspoons dried shrimps
3 stalks lemon grass, crushed
1 teaspoon ground coriander
4 tablespoons or 1 bunch fresh coriander leaves, chopped
juice and grated rind of 2 limes
3 fresh kaffir lime leaves (optional)

Combine all the ingredients and liquidise or process to a smooth paste in a food processor.

This can be added to any ingredients you like, for example lightly fried strips of breast of chicken, or strips of beef, green and red peppers and onions, baby sweet corn or anything else that takes your fancy. Serve with Thai fragrant rice.

I've enclosed one of my favourite recipes (Thai, of course!) which I hope will help make your book a huge success and which will raise loads of money for the Khao Lak Community Appeal.

Best wishes

Lorraine Kelly
LK Today

Lorraine Kelly is the presenter of her own GMTV show called *LK Today*, which goes out live four days a week. She also co-presents ITV's *This Morning* every Monday and Friday and writes a weekly column for the *Sun* newspaper and the *Scottish Post*.

Felicity Kendall
ROSEMARY POTATOES

Serves 2

450g (1lb) small new potatoes
2 tablespoons olive oil
1 tablespoons butter
fresh sprigs rosemary
2 garlic cloves, chopped
sea salt
freshly ground black pepper

A much admired
British actress of the stage and
screen, Felicity became a household
name in 1975 with the TV sitcom *The Good
Life*. Her stage career blossomed during the
1980s and 1990s. Her most recent TV work
is as Rosemary Boxer in the ITV murder
mystery series *Rosemary and Thyme*.

Boil the new potatoes in their skin in salted water until they are cooked. Heat the olive oil and butter in a frying pan. Throw in the rosemary and garlic and fry for a couple of minutes. Put the cooked whole small new potatoes into the pan (if larger than a walnut slice them). Sprinkle with sea salt and freshly ground pepper and fry until brown and crisp.

If you are not going to eat them immediately they can be kept in a warm oven quite comfortably.

Charles Kennedy MP
BEEF CASSEROLE

Serves 4

The Right Honourable Charles Kennedy, British politician is the Liberal Democrats' MP for Ross, Skye and Lochaber. He has been leader of the Liberal Democrats since 9 August 1999.

900g (2 lb) stewing steak, cubed
25g (1 oz) seasoned flour
50g (2 oz) butter
1 large onion, finely chopped
2 pints beef stock
1 bay leaf
¼ pint soured cream

Pre-heat oven to 170°C / 325°F / Gas mark 3

Coat the beef cubes in seasoned flour. Melt the butter in a flameproof casserole dish. Add beef cubes to the butter and brown on all sides. As the cubes brown remove from casserole. Add onion to the casserole and fry until softened. Return the beef to the casserole dish. Stir in the beef stock and add bay leaf. Bring to the boil, cover and transfer to oven. Cook for 1½ hours.

After the initial 1½ hours stir the casserole, re-cover and cook for a further ½ hour. Remove bay leaf.

Finally spoon the sour cream over casserole before serving.

Chris Kenworthy
RACK OF LAMB with BEANS & ROASTED ONIONS

Serves 6

2 racks of lamb, trimmed and prepared by your butcher
2 fat garlic cloves, sliced
2 wands of rosemary, freshly picked
2 medium sized red onions, peeled and chopped into quarters
2 x 420g cans of flageolet beans
2 tablespoons of olive oil
Salt and freshly milled black pepper

Chris Kenworthy was, until his retirement, a show business writer in Fleet Street, working for newspapers and magazines. Now, he writes adventure novels and westerns from his home in West Sussex.

Heat the oven to gas mark 220°C / 425 °F / Gas mark 7

With a sharp knife, make a slit between the skin and the meat of the racks of lamb and slide into it slices of garlic and a stem of rosemary so as to flavour the whole rack. Wipe down with olive oil and grind pepper and salt on the skin.

Into a deep roasting tin wiped down with olive oil, place the flageolet beans and onions, and drizzle oil over the onions to prevent them scorching.

Place the lamb on a wire mesh tray above the beans and onions, and place high in the oven for a half hour for pink meat and forty minutes for better done meat.

Slice through the joint to separate the cutlets and serve immediately.

Add mashed potatoes mixed with celeriac if you feel you need more, but beware! This dish is satisfying by itself.

Delicious with a good Beaujolais.

Mark Knopfler & Kitty Aldridge
SEARED SCALLOPS
with MIXED SALAD LEAVES

Serves 4   preparation time: 15 minutes   Cooking time: 10 minutes

(You will need approximately half a medium red cabbage and a quarter of a medium savoy cabbage). If preferred you can use bean shoots, watercress and cooked/cooled green beans instead of cabbage and cucumber.

32 scallops (1.3kg) roe removed
2 Lebanese cucumbers (260g)
3 cups (240g) finely shredded red cabbage
2 cups (160g) finely shredded savoy cabbage
half cup coarsely chopped fresh chives
2 tablespoons toasted sesame seeds

Honey Soy Dressing

2 tablespoons soy sauce
2 tablespoons lemon juice
2 teaspoons sesame oil
1 tablespoon honey
1 clove garlic, crushed
a quarter cup (60ml) peanut oil

A fantastic British guitarist, singer and songwriter, Mark is best known as the lead guitarist and vocalist of his band *Dire Straits*, but has also made albums as a solo performer. He is married to Kitty Aldridge, actress and author.

1. Make honey soy dressing by mixing ingredients together.

2. Sear scallops in large, heated, oiled frying pan, in batches, until browned both sides and cooked as desired.

3. Using a veg peeler slice the cucumbers into ribbons. Mix the cucumber in a large bowl with cabbages, chives, seeds and ¾ of the dressing.

4. Divide salad among serving plates; top with the scallops, drizzle with the remaining dressing.

Warning: Do not give this dish to anyone without checking whether they are allergic to peanuts.

Gabby Logan
SALMON CHOWDER

Serves 4

fish stock (obviously homemade is best but you can buy fish stock from the supermarket)
2 large potatoes, diced
4 organic salmon fillets
6–8 rashers of bacon
packet of mange tout
340ml (12 fl oz) of pouring cream
good handful of fresh, chopped parsley

Fry the bacon in a pan and then remove and cut into strips.

Return to the pan with fish stock and the diced potatoes and cook for 20–30 minutes, until the potatoes are tender.

Add the salmon and mange tout and cook on medium heat for 5–10 minutes.

3–4 minutes before the end add the cream and season to taste. Add chopped parsley and stir in just before serving.

Serve with sourdough or crusty bread.

Delicious !

Gabby Logan is a British television sports presenter, a woman who knows about football. She is married to former Scotland International Rugby player Kenny Logan and on 28 July 2005 she gave birth to twins.

Dame Vera Lynn
CHICKEN (or TURKEY) BOOBS

Serves 2

2 chicken or turkey breasts
1 large onion
2 chopped tomatoes
6 finely cut small mushrooms
¼ pint chicken stock to taste
garlic and herbs to taste

Saute a large onion and when softened add the breasts. Add the chopped tomatoes, then the finely cut small mushrooms. Add a little stock according to your taste, to form a sauce. Put on lid and simmer until tender. Add garlic and herbs to suit your taste.

A wonderful British singer whose career flourished during World War II, she was affectionately nicknamed "The Forces Sweetheart". Dame Vera Lynn is best known for the popular song *We'll Meet Again*. During the England VE ceremonies in 2005 she made a surprise appearance giving a speech praising the Veterans. In 1969 Dame Vera was given an OBE, and in 1975, a DBE.

Alex Mackay
GRILLED PRAWNS
with TOMATO & BASIL BUTTER

Prawns are sold in different sizes. I prefer their flesh to that of lobster or langouste as they are the easiest to use, cut and make bisque with. This is a recipe for seafood lovers who enjoy eating with their hands. I tried it first using olive oil, which is also lovely, but the butter just gave that little extra decadence. Have some bread handy that you can pull the middle out of to dip in whatever is left of the butter.

Serves 4

12 large raw tiger prawns, shells on
2 large garlic cloves, peeled and chopped
2 strips dried orange zest, crushed
salt and cayenne pepper
½ teaspoon tomato concentrate
2 very ripe Roma tomatoes, seeded and chopped
4 sprigs fresh basil, leaves picked from stalks, chopped
100g (3½ oz) unsalted butter, softened

Preheat your grill to its highest setting.

Split the tiger prawns down the centre of their backs, remove the intestinal cord and discard. If they have any coral, spoon this out and reserve it for the butter. Lay them out, cut flesh side up, on a tray that will fit under your grill.

Mix the garlic and orange zest with a little salt, add the tomato concentrate, tomatoes, basil and butter. Add as much spice as you like with the cayenne pepper and smear over the prawns.

Grill them for about 6–8 minutes. Check that they are ready by lifting up the thickest part of the prawns near the head: it should be pinkish white and no longer transparent.

Serve as hot as possible and make sure there are plenty of finger bowls and napkins.

Recipes and photographs fom *Cooking in Provence*. Text © 2003 Alex Mackay.
Photographs © 2003 Peter Knab. Reproduced by permission of the publishers Headline Book Publishing Ltd.

Alex Mackay
GRILLED SEA BREAM
with PISTOU of SHELLFISH

I used marbré, the very beautiful marbled sea bream, for the photo, but any type of sea bream would be fine. The silver-blue daurade royale, the daurade rose known in Italy as bocca d'oro for its golden mouth, and the pink-gold pagre are often stuffed with fennel and grilled whole or cooked in crusts of sea salt. This mixture is a type of soupe au pistou with shellfish added. The pistou mixture can be cooked a few hours in advance up to the point of adding the shellfish. Should you find fresh beans difficult to obtain, just omit them.

Serves 4

4 large fillets of sea bream, each 150g (5½ oz) plus a little extra virgin olive oil for grilling
salt and freshly ground black pepper

Pistou of shellfish

1 large red pepper, seeded and cut into large dice
50ml (2fl oz) extra virgin olive oil
1 small white onion, peeled and roughly chopped
2 garlic cloves, peeled and cut into large dice
500g (1lb 2oz) fresh white haricot beans, 250g (9oz) shelled weight
1 large courgette, cut into large dice
24 clams, well rinsed
24 mussels, de-bearded and rinsed
3 Roma tomatoes, seeded and chopped
1 small bunch fresh basil, leaves picked from the stalks, chopped

New Zealand born Alex is a well respected cookery writer and teacher. He holds regular monthly cookery workshops at Delia Smith's famous restaurant at Norwich City Football Club. He once ran his own cookery school in Provence – the inspiration behind his book *Cooking in Provence.* He also ran the cookery school at the *Le Manoir aux Quat Saisons.*

Preheat your grill to its highest setting.

Sweat the diced red pepper in the oil for 5 minutes, then add the onion and garlic and sweat for 5 minutes more. Add the beans and just enough water to cover, then simmer for 25 minutes until the beans are soft and the liquid has all but gone. Transfer the mixture to a large shallow pan with a tight-fitting lid and add the courgettes, clams and mussels. Cover and cook quickly for about 5 minutes until the shellfish open (discard any that don't).

While the shellfish are cooking, lay the fillets of bream on a tray, brush them with olive oil, season well and grill for 6–8 minutes. Mix the chopped tomatoes and basil with the shellfish mixture and serve with the bream.

Alex Mackay
STRAWBERRIES & LEMON CURD
with FILO PASTRY

Lemons and berries are real symbols of Provence. The big, gnarled, untreated lemons have a tarty fresh look and flavour that perks you up enormously. As for the strawberries, in season, particularly when warm from the sun, they have a corruptingly decadent fragrance. I've combined the two here with a little crispy filo to make a dessert that has everything: sweet, sour and crisp. Not only that, you can prepare it at least 12 hours in advance and just assemble at the last minute.

Serves 4

4 sheets of filo pastry
50g (2 oz) unsalted butter, melted
icing sugar for dusting

lemon curd
1 large egg
1 large egg yolk
finely grated zest and juice of 1 lemon,
about 50ml (2fl oz) juice
50g (2 oz) icing sugar
50g (2 oz) butter

the strawberries
450g (1lb) strawberries, stems
removed
100g (3½ oz) icing sugar

Preheat your oven to 180°C /350°F / Gas mark 4.
Double up the sheets of filo pastry so that you have two rectangles of two layers.
Brush them well with melted butter. Cut eight 12 x 6cm (4½ x 2½ inch) rectangles from the large rectangles and put them flat on a baking tray. Dredge them with plenty of icing sugar and bake for 6–8 minutes until golden and caramelised on top. Store in a dry place.
To make the lemon curd, mix the eggs and icing sugar in a thick-bottomed, stainless steel saucepan. Add the lemon zest, juice and butter and whisk over a medium heat until it thickens to the texture of a thick custard. Transfer the curd to a bowl, put a piece of clingfilm directly on the surface to stop a skin forming and leave it to cool. This can easily be made two days in advance.
Cut 150g (5 oz) of the strawberries into small pieces and put them into a saucepan with the icing sugar and 2 tablespoons of water. Cook this over a low heat for a couple of minutes until the sugar dissolves. Turn up the heat and simmer for 5 minutes until thick. Leave it to cool for a while, then halve or quarter the remaining strawberries and toss them through it.
Build each millefeuille, first starting with a little lemon curd, followed by a filo rectangle, more lemon curd, the strawberries then another filo rectangle. Repeat this once more, then make the other three.

Michelle Magorian
TOM'S CHEESY PASTA

This has been my older son's favourite recipe for years. We call it CHEESY PASTA.

Put four generous handfuls of pasta (I use organic wholewheat fusilli) into a small saucepan.

Using a cheese slicer, slice thin layers of cheddar cheese and cut up enough ham into small pieces to fill a quarter of large side plate. (I use wafer thin smoked ham.)

Line the base of a large flat based bowl with half the layers of cheese.

Pour boiling water into the pasta and bring it to the boil again. Turn the ring down to between 3 and 4 and turn the oven on at 140°C / 275°F / Gas mark 1 to warm.

Simmer the pasta for eight minutes. Drain and pour the pasta into the cheese lined bowl. Sprinkle the ham on top of the pasta and spread the remaining layers of cheese on top so that it covers it.

Put into the oven for 7 - 8 minutes if it's half fat cheddar and 4 minutes if it's full fat cheddar.

Take out of the oven, lift out the pasta with two large spoons and heap it into a bowl. The cheese should be gooey and melted throughout the pasta from top to bottom.

Not very exotic really!

My favourite recipe is:

STIR FRY FRESH VEGETABLES

Michelle Magorian
is both an accomplished actress
and writer. Her first book, *Goodnight
Mr Tom*, propelled her to fame and is widely
regarded as a modern classic. Her second book,
Back Home, has also been very successful
and both of them have been adapted for
television, with *Goodnight Mr Tom*
winning several TV Awards.

Onion, garlic, leeks, mushrooms, peppers, cabbage etc. sprinkled with tamari (or soya sauce) with brown rice and freshly roasted peanuts sprinkled on top, accompanied by a glass of cool, dry white wine.

I used to make this for myself every Saturday afternoon, slicing up the vegetables while listening to the Radio 3 Jazz programme or a Jazz CD.

Hope this helps. Love Michelle

Warning: Do not give this dish to anyone without checking whether they are allergic to peanuts.

Sir John & Dame Norma Major
MONKFISH, PRAWNS & MUSHROOMS
in a LIME & DILL SAUCE

900g monkfish*
2 teaspoons olive oil
salt and pepper
juice of 3 limes
zest of 1 lime
25g finely chopped onion
125g peeled prawns
300ml double cream
50g unsalted butter
125g puff pastry
1 teaspoon fresh dill (chopped)
125g oyster mushrooms

The Right Honourable Sir John Major served in the Cabinets of Margaret Thatcher as Chief Secretary to the Treasury, Foreign Secretary and Chancellor of the Exchequer. He became Conservative Party Leader and was Prime Minister from 1990–1997. He retired from politics in the 2001 General Election and was knighted in 2005.

His wife, Dame Norma Major DBE wrote a book, *Chequers: The Prime Minister's Country House and Its History*. She was created a Dame Commander of the Order of the British Empire in the 1999 Queen's Birthday Honours, in recognition of her charity work.

Prepare 4 rounds of puff pastry and cook until golden brown.

Cut trimmed monkfish fillets into even-sized pieces.

Heat 1 teaspoon of oil and sauté monkfish until cooked, remove and keep warm.

Add onions to pan and cook quickly without colour.

Add lime juice and zest and reduce by half.

Add cream, boil until thickened, add 1 teaspoon chopped dill.

Remove from heat, whisk in cubes of cold butter.

Cook mushrooms in remaining oil, add prawns and heat through.

Place puff pastry circles on 4 plates, cover with prawns and mushrooms.

Place monkfish escalopes over prawns and mushrooms and pour a ring of the sauce around the escalopes.

Decorate with sprigs of dill for garnish.

*Any firm fish can be substituted for, or combined with, the monkfish.

Aggie Mackenzie
MY MUM'S SHORTBREAD

This is my mum's recipe for shortbread…delicious! Not at all Thai, but of course, very Scottish.

200g (7 oz) plain flour, sifted
50g (2 oz) cornflour
175g (6 oz) unsalted butter, softened
75g (3 oz) golden caster sugar
A little extra sugar to sprinkle.

Put everything in a food processor until it just comes together. Wrap in clingfilm and chill for 30 minutes. Heat oven to 190°C / 375°F / Gas mark 5.

Divide the dough into 2 and roll out each to a circle of about 6½ inches in diameter.

Put each into a 7 inch sandwich tin (so that the paste sits short of the sides by about half an inch). Prick all over well with a fork and bake in the oven for about 35–40 minutes or until golden brown.

Sprinkle with sugar and cut while warm.

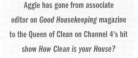

Aggie has gone from associate editor on *Good Housekeeping* magazine to the Queen of Clean on Channel 4's hit show *How Clean is your House?*

James Martin
THAI ROASTED CRAB RISOTTO

Makes 4 portions

275g (10 oz) arborio rice
300 ml (½ pint) fresh chicken stock
300 ml (½ pint) fresh fish stock
450g (1 lb) fresh white and dark crab meat
100 ml (3½ fl oz) Muscat white wine
2 tablespoons Mascarpone
50 ml (2 fl oz) double cream
1 stick of lemon grass
15g (½ oz) flat leaf parsley and coriander
2 shallots
2 garlic cloves
110g (4 oz) fresh Parmesan Reggiano
25g (1 oz) butter
2 green chillies
3 Kaffir lime leaves
1 pinch of curry powder
Thai green curry paste
1 fresh lime
olive oil
seasoning

1. Peel and finely chop the garlic and shallot and place into a warm pan with the butter. Sweat for about a minute. Add the rice and then the wine. Before adding the stock add the chopped green chillies, curry powder, curry paste, crushed lemon grass and lime leaves. Then add the warm chicken and fish stock mixed, a ladle at a time while simmering until the rice is cooked. It should take about 13 to 15 minutes stirring all the time.

2. Once the rice is cooked add the mascarpone and cream and all the chopped herbs. Add the crab meat and parmesan. Adjust with more stock and cream if need be, add the lime juice and season well. Place in the centre of the plates and top with a little chilli oil and some more parmesan.

James Martin
THAI CHICKEN CAKES
with SWEET CHILLI SAUCE

Serves 4   Preparation time 10 minutes   Cooking time 5 minutes

2 chicken breasts, cubed
1 garlic clove, roughly chopped
1cm knob fresh root ginger, roughly chopped
1 small onion, roughly chopped
2 tablespoons coriander, chopped
1 green chilli, roughly chopped
salt & freshly ground black pepper
2 tablespoons olive oil

To serve

Sweet chilli sauce
1 spring onion, finely sliced

1. Place the chicken, garlic, ginger, onion, coriander and chilli in a food processor and season to taste with salt and pepper. Blitz for 15–20 seconds.

2. Shape the chicken mixture into small cakes.

3. Heat the olive oil in a frying pan over a moderate heat and fry the chicken cakes until golden.

4. Serve immediately, with sweet chilli sauce and a finely sliced spring onion.

James was brought up in a farmhouse in Yorkshire where his father ran the catering side of Castle Howard. He began his formal training at Scarborough Technical College. His TV career began in 1996 on the popular TV show *Ready Steady Cook* and he has been a regular ever since. He has featured in many TV programmes, his latest is a TV series *A Castle in the Country* filmed at Glamis Castle. He has a number of cookbooks to his name such as *Delicious* based on recipes from his deli in Winchester and his latest – *Easy British Dinners.*

James Martin
CRAB & SWEETCORN SPRING ROLLS

Serves 4

300g (10¾ oz) white crab meat
3 tablespoons mustard mayonnaise
100g (3 ½ oz) cooked sweetcorn, patted dry
1 tablespoon chopped fresh basil
1 tablespoon chopped fresh coriander
12 rice paper wrappers or sheets of filo pastry (each about 23cm square)
2 egg yolks, beaten with 1 teaspoon water
100ml (3½ fl oz) classic vinaigrette
1 tablespoon fresh harissa
sunflower oil for deep frying
salad leaves to serve
sea salt & freshly ground black pepper

1. Finely flake the crab meat with a fork, removing any stray pieces of shell or cartilage as you go. Season well and mix the mustard mayonnaise, sweetcorn, basil and coriander.

2. Place a rice paper wrapper or sheet of filo at an angle on a board so that one of the corners point towards you. Brush around the edges with the egg-yolk wash. Spoon about a tablespoon of the crab filling in a line near the top corner. Fold over the top corner and roll towards you a little, then fold in the sides and continue to roll up. Place on a non-stick tray. Repeat with the remaining filling, wrappers or filo and egg wash to make 12 rolls in all. Lightly brush with the remaining egg wash and chill for about 30 minutes.

3. Meanwhile, whisk the vinaigrette with the harissa and set aside.

4. Pour oil to a depth of 6–7cm into a deep pan and heat to a temperature of around 180°C / 350°F, or until a small piece of white bread turns golden brown in about 30 seconds. Deep fry the rolls, four at a time, for 3–4 minutes or until golden brown and crisp on all sides. Reheat the oil in between batches. Drain on kitchen paper towels. Serve warm and crisp, with the harissa vinaigrette as a dipping sauce and a little salad.

James Martin
CLEAR THAI SALMON & LOBSTER SOUP

2 red chillies plus extra for garnish
4 garlic cloves
50g (2 oz) galangal or ginger
1 teaspoon coriander seeds
20g (¾ oz) fresh coriander
50ml sesame oil
250g (9 oz) fillet salmon, with skin on but no bones, cut into bite-sized pieces
700g (1½ lb) lobster
2 limes
750ml (1¼ –1½ pints) fresh fish stock (available in small tubs from supermarkets)
50ml (2 fl oz) Asian fish sauce
200g (7 oz) dried vermicelli noodles
fresh mint and coriander
6 spring onions
Soy Sauce

Cook the lobster in the fish stock for 11 minutes per pound. Remove from the stock and remove all the meat. Crush the shells and coriander seeds and add to the soup. Skim off the stock and discard the bones once cool. Cook the noodles in boiling water, drain and place in the middle of the serving bowl, piled high. Add the salmon, chopped mint, chilli, galangal or ginger and garlic to the soup and cook for 3-4 minutes and then pour over the noodles. Garnish the top of the noodles with spring onions, lobster meat, salmon and herbs. Finish the soup with limes, sesame oil, fish sauce, coriander leaves and diced chilli.

It's great to be part of something that is such a worthwhile cause. It is amazing how something can devastate the lives of so many. This book has my full support, enjoy the recipes and thank you for buying it.

James Martin

Davina McCall
VEGGIE SOUP

I love this because it's sooooooooooo easy and fab for a winter's evening.

1 onion
olive oil
2 cloves garlic, crushed
3 potatoes (or 8 new potatoes in their skin)
3 sweet potatoes, peeled and cut into chunks
3 large carrots
a handful of baby button mushrooms (whole)
1 red pepper, roughly chopped
½ cauliflower, chopped
3 leeks, sliced
10 broccoli florets
tomato paste
vegetable or chicken stock cube (fresh stock if you have it)
1 tin Campbells cream of tomato soup (optional… a bit naughty)
seasoning

Davina McCall is one of Britain's most popular television presenters. She is best known for working as a presenter on MTV and presenting the UK Edition of *Big Brother.*

Roughly chop the onion and garlic and sauté in some olive oil. Then bung in the mushrooms and the peppers for a couple of minutes, closely followed by all the other veggies. Coat them with oil, give them a good season with salt and pepper and add 2 tablespoons of tomato paste. Then add the liquid, just enough boiling water to cover the veggies. It is at this point that I sometimes add half a tin of 'Campbell's'. It is a bit naughty as it kind of detracts from the homemade thingy but it does make it very yummy!

Then put the lid on… keep it on a very low heat and cook for about an hour stirring occasionally. Then, when everything is cooked through, mash it and season to taste.

I usually make loads and it gets better every time it's heated. Sometimes I'll add some rice or noodles.

Hope you like it!!!!

Tamara Mellon
POULET ST. BARTH

Serves 6

A

1 kg chicken breasts

Tamara Mellon is the founder and
president of the world famous Jimmy
Choo Shoe Company.

B

1 red or white onion
1 yellow, 1 red and 1 green pepper, cut into tiny cubes
1 carrot, cut into tiny cubes
1 garlic clove finely chopped

C

3 teaspoons of French wholegrain mustard
¼ litre of crème fraîche
200 ml of veal stock

Sauté A in butter, allowing chicken to take colour.

Sauté B separately in 3 parts olive oil to 1 part butter, until soft but not coloured.

Add A to B and simmer for 10 minutes, shaking from time to time.

Add C, cook for 10–15 mins on medium heat.

Serve with chopped spring onions and rice.

*This was our favourite dish in St Barth's at Christmas cooked by our young French chef
Manu. He did the best home-cooked comfort food but it never felt heavy or fattening. We'd
run back from the beach every day desperate for lunch. When he asked us what we wanted to
serve at a dinner party we threw for Nick Rhodes, his girlfriend Meredith, Tamara Beckwith
and her boyfriend, Giorgio Veroni, Kate Reardon, Catherine Prevost and her husband
Andreas Heeschen, we asked for Poulet St Barth. Everyone had second helpings.*

Ismail Merchant
SPAGHETTI aur MACHLI ROBERTO SILVI
(Robert Silvi's Spaghetti & Tuna)

Preparation time: 45 minutes

Serves 4–6

3 tablespoons olive oil
1 whole head of garlic, the cloves separated, peeled and chopped
2 red bell peppers, seeded and chopped
1 x 355g (12½ oz) can tuna in olive oil
1 third tube anchovy paste
¾ large can tomatoes, chopped
large handful of chopped fresh parsley
salt to taste
2 lbs cooked spaghetti

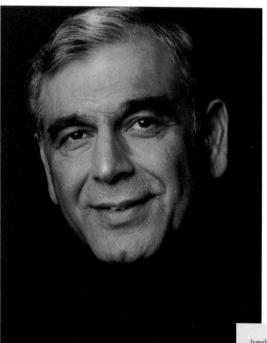

Combine in a heavy saucepan the olive oil, garlic, bell peppers, tuna with its oil, anchovy paste, and tomatoes with their liquid. Cook over medium heat, stirring often so the tomatoes do not burn, for about 25 or 30 minutes. When the sauce is ready, add parsley and salt. Toss well into freshly cooked spaghetti.

This dish is traditionally eaten in Italy on Fridays when Catholics used to be prohibited from eating meat. The prohibition has been lifted but the tradition lingers on.

Ismail Merchant was an Indian born film producer, best known for his long collaboration with director James Ivory. Together they founded *Merchant Ivory Productions*, and they have a place in the Guinness Book of World Records for the longest partnership in independent cinema history. He was fond of cooking and wrote several cook books. Sadly Ismail Merchant died on 25 May 2005.

Ismail Merchant

BHUNA GOSHT
(Pan Roasted Lamb)

Preparation time: 1½ hours, plus marinating

Serves 12

2 kg (4½ lbs) boneless lean leg of lamb (about 3.2 kg (7lbs) before boning and trimming)
2 tablespoons finely chopped, fresh ginger root
3 fresh hot green chillies, chopped with seeds
1 tablespoon finely chopped garlic
1½ tablespoons chopped coriander leaves
juice of 1 lemon
salt to taste
1 teaspoon ground black pepper
1 tablespoon vegetable oil

Cut the meat into 1½ inch cubes and place in a bowl. Combine the ginger, chillies, garlic, coriander, lemon juice, salt, pepper and oil, and mix with the lamb. Set aside to marinate in the refrigerator for at least 1 hour or until you are ready to cook.

Heat the oven to 180°C / 350°F / Gas mark 4.

Put the lamb and its marinade in a shallow roasting pan measuring about 9 x 13 inches. Bake, uncovered for 1¼ hours without stirring. The lamb should be tender with plenty of pan juices.

Serve with Basmati rice and a curly endive salad.

Ismail Merchant
'QUARTET' PHAI KA SALAD
('Quartet' Fruit Salad)

This is a dessert served in the film 'Quartet'

Preparation time: 15 minutes, plus minimum 2 hours chilling.

Serves 8-10

425 ml (15 fl oz) good red Beaujolais wine
4 teaspoons sugar
2 cinnamon sticks, broken in pieces
juice of 4 lemons
900g (2lb) ripe strawberries, hulled
4 kiwi fruit, peeled and sliced
2 apples, cored and cubed
450g (1lb) cherries, seeded
1½ lb ripe peaches, peeled, seeded and sliced
4 sprigs fresh mint, stems removed

Pour the wine into a large bowl and add the sugar, cinnamon and lemon juice. Prepare the rest of the ingredients in the order listed, stirring them immediately into the wine mixture.

Chill the mixture in the refrigerator at least 2 hours before serving.

*Though this salad is perfect on its own, you can gild the lily serving it with crème fraîche.

Keith Michell
BROWN RICE & CHINESE STYLE VEGETABLES

Serves 4

3 cups of cooked short-grained brown rice (for cooking rice facing page)
2 tablespoons of olive oil or sesame oil
4 medium-sized mushrooms (shitake if available)
1 large onion, sliced thin
1 medium carrot, sliced
3 cups shredded cabbage
1 cup water (or vegetable stock)
2 cups winter squash, peeled and diced
½ cubic inch fresh ginger, grated
1 cup mange tout
1 heaped teaspoon kuzu (similar to cornflour)
½ cup apple juice
2 teaspoons tamari (naturally fermented soy sauce)
2 teaspoons roasted sesame seeds to garnish
chopped parsley or spring onions to garnish

Australian born, acclaimed actor of the stage and screen. Keith Michell has starred in much lauded London and Broadway productions of *La Cage Aux Folles, Man of La Mancha* and *Irma La Douce*. His films include *House of Cards, Dangerous Exile, Henry VIII and his Six Wives* and *The Executioner.*

He is the author of *Keith Michell's Practically Macriobiotic Cookbook.*

1. Lightly sauté onions in the oil.

2. Stir in carrot, cabbage, mushrooms, squash and grated ginger. Add water and bring to the boil. Cover and simmer for 5 minutes.

3. Add Mange tout and continue to simmer for a further 5 minutes.

4. Dissolve kuzu (corn flour) in the apple juice and add tamari soy sauce. Stir into the cooking vegetables until the mixture thickens.

5. Serve vegetables over the rice and garnish with sesame seeds and parsley or spring onions.

"Brown Rice should be the staple of your diet. It is an excellent food, low in fat and rich in vitamins and minerals" says nutritionist Nan Bronfen. *Rice, like wheat and many other cultivated grains is native to the dry valleys of Central Asia. Interestingly enough early Chinese civilization didn't know rice at all – their staple grains were sorghum, wheat, millet in the north and yams in the swampy south. Aquatic rice is thought to have become established in India and to have reached China by 2000 B.C. spreading from there to Indonesia. Rice did not play a particularly important part in Japanese diet until as late as the seventeenth century. Today more than half the world's population lives mainly on rice and it is incredible that rice eaten in many overpopulated areas should be commercially 'refined' white rice deprived of nourishing protein, calcium, iron, B vitamins etc., lost when the valuable outer layers are removed.*

Whole grain brown rice is referred to as 'soul food' by Georges Ohsawa who introduced macrobiotics, 'it has the perfect balance of yin and yang'. It is an important, central part of your diet. It is convenient for daily use and will help calm you when you are feeling edgy – usually from dietary overindulgence! – or in times of stress or sickness. Learning to cook it well is one of the first macrobiotic lessons. The harder, more compact short-grained rice is better suited for eating in cooler climates. Long grained rice is better for warmer regions and hot weather. Cooked rice can be stored in a cool place or can be refrigerated, reheated, steamed, baked or fried, made into rice croquettes, used in soups, salads, even desserts or breads.

Make sure your rice is whole grain. Use organically grown if possible – it should say 'organic' on the package. If it doesn't it isn't! Whole grain takes longer to cook than commercial 'white' rice. The cooking time can be spent preparing the vegetables or sauce to go with it.

To cook brown rice:

1 cup of whole grain brown rice
3 cups water
pinch of ground Kombu (or sea salt)

1. Wash the rice. Place in a ceramic, stainless steel, cast iron or enamel pot – preferably with a heavy lid. Add water and kombu (or salt). It adds to the flavour and texture if you then soak for 2 or 3 hours. Bring to the boil.

2. Allow to boil vigorously for five minutes, cover with lid, lower the heat and simmer gently for 30 to 40 minutes, or until water has disappeared. Do not stir or disturb the grain. If the heat is low it shouldn't burn.

3. Turn off heat and, still covered, allow to stand for 10 minutes or until ready. Use a wooden ladle or spoon.

Practically Macrobiotic by Keith Michell   Publisher Inner Traditions 3rd edtion 2000

Cliff Michelmore
SMOKED HADDOCK BALLS

225g (½ lb) smoked haddock
300ml (½ pint) milk
25g (1 oz) butter
25g (1 oz) plain flour
110g (4 oz) breadcrumbs — dried white crumbs for coating
1 egg, beaten
salt, pepper, curry powder

Simmer the fish in milk …save the liquid. Flake the fish and set aside.

To make sauce with the fish milk – melt the butter in a saucepan. Stir in the flour and cook for 1–2 minutes. Take the pan off the heat and gradually stir in the milk to get a smooth sauce. Return to the heat, stirring all the time. Bring to the boil and gently simmer for 8–10 minutes. Stir in fish and seasoning.

Leave to cool before forming into balls.

Dip in egg and crumbs.

Deep fry and then serve with tartare sauce……delicious!!

GRANDPA'S CHEAT

Serves 4

10fl oz whipped cream
4 crunchie bars

Put the crunchie bars in a bag and crush them with a rolling pin. Mix it with the whipped cream and then put it in the freezer.

The kids will think you are a genius!!

Clifford Michelmore C.B.E., a British television presenter and producer. He is best known for the BBC1 programme *Tonight*, which he presented from 1957 to 1965. Notably, he also hosted the BBC's coverage of the Apollo Moon landings and the 1964, 1966 and 1970 UK General Elections.

Michelmore was a RAF Squadron Leader during World War II, and began his broadcasting career on British Forces Network radio. After the war, he worked for BBC radio and television on a freelance basis, initially as a sports commentator, then as a news reporter and as a producer of children's programmes.

On 4 March 1950, he married his British Forces Network Colleague Jean Metcalfe; they went on to have two children.

From 1955 to 1957 Michelmore presented the BBC TV programme *Highlight*, a current affairs show with a reputation for hard-hitting interviews. On 18th February 1957 he was made anchorman of the BBC TV's new topical weekday evening show *Tonight*. In 1958 Cliff was awarded the accolade of Television Personality of the Year by the Guild of Television Producers. When Tonight finished its run in 1965, Michelmore hosted a BBC1 series called *24 hours*, which ran until 1968. He was a regular presenter on BBC1's *Holiday* programme from 1969 to 1986, and has presented numerous other shows for the BBC, ITV and BBC radio.

Cliff now lives near his daughter and her family and is enjoying his retirement reading, doing crosswords and indulging his grandchildren.

David Neilson
CREAMY VEGETABLE LASAGNE

Make some ratatouille with courgettes, onions, peppers, tomato purée, freshly crushed garlic and a couple of tins of tomatoes.

Put a layer of lasagne (preferably fresh) in the bottom of a baking dish. Add a layer of ratatouille followed by a covering of cheese sauce, a splash of red wine, a dash of cream, some freshly chopped parsley, freshly grated parmesan and black pepper.

Continue with these layers until the baking dish is full, finishing with the lasagne sheets covered.

Cook for 50 minutes. 180°C / 350°F / Gas mark 4.

Serve with garlic bread made with herbs, green salad and a bottle of red wine.

Sorry I can't list all the ingredients properly. Just try this out for yourselves and you'll see it's really delicious.

David Neilson
trained at the Central School
of Speech and Drama. He has worked
as a Theatre Director, running the *Little Theatre Company* in Bristol. He currently plays the role of Roy Cropper in *Coronation Street.*

HRH Princess Michael of Kent
COLD TERRINE of HARDBOILED EGGS

I love to make a cold terrine of hard boiled eggs – grated, mixed with grated onion, some chopped parsley, mixed with a tin of Campbell's consomme, (must be Campbell's as it will jellify) add some cream and put it in the fridge to chill and become aspic. This is also delicious and easy.

SPINACH SOUP

The other thing I used to have success with was a spinach soup. Take a packet of frozen chopped or pureed spinach, defrost, add chicken stock, butter, garlic, mix and then add sour cream. Serve chilled in the summer.

Yum. Why do I like it? Because it is easy…

Her Royal Highness Princess Michael of Kent is a member of the British Royal Family by marriage to The Queen's first cousin. She is also a lecturer and has published three best selling history books.

Nicolino's Restaurant, Emsworth
RICOTTA CHEESE CAKE
with Limoncello liqueur and served with marinated strawberries

Serves 6

400g fresh strawberries, hulled and cut in half
75ml Limoncello liqueur
75g caster sugar
250g amaretti biscuits
100g plain chocolate, chopped
50g butter

Filling

600g Ricotta cheese
150g caster sugar
50g mixed peel
50ml Strega liqueur
4 egg yolks
4 egg whites
cocoa powder to decorate
(Limoncello is a sweet liqueur made from the peel of the famous lemons which grow on the Amalfi Coast. Strega is an Italian liqueur fermented in oak and made from 70 herbs and spices including saffron, which gives it its bright yellow colour).

First make the marinated strawberries:

In a bowl pour in Limoncello and the sugar, mix well. Add the strawberries and mix. Leave in a refrigerator for two hours.

Preheat oven to 160°C / 325°F / Gas mark 3.

Grease a 9 inch cake tin.

Crush the amaretti biscuits. Melt the chocolate and butter in a bowl set over a pan of simmering water, and then mix with the crumbs.

Spoon the mixture into the tin, press down.

In a large bowl beat the yolks and sugar. Add the Ricotta, mixed peel, Strega liqueur and beat together.

Beat the egg whites to soft peak then fold in to the cheese and egg mixture. Pour over the base of the cake tin and bake for 50 minutes until firm. Leave to cool.

When chilled decorate with cocoa powder on top and serve with the marinated strawberries.

Drink Strega liqueur.

Jamie Oliver
THAI MARINATED STEAMED SALMON

serves 4

4 x 200g pieces of salmon fillet
½ a bottle of soy sauce
3 thumb-sized pieces of ginger, sliced
2 sticks of lemongrass
a handful of coriander leaves, chopped
2 red chillies, sliced
sea salt and freshly ground black pepper
6 baby leeks or 3 small leeks, trimmed and cut into quarters
extra virgin olive oil

Place the pieces of salmon in a large flat plastic or china dish. Cover with the soy sauce, ginger, lemongrass, coriander and chillies, and season. Leave to marinate for about an hour – the salmon will become almost waxy in appearance.

Place the leeks in the bottom of a large steamer. Cover with the salmon and the rest of the marinade. Place the steamer over a large pan of boiling water and pour over any remaining soy sauce, which can drip into the water below.

Cover and steam for 10 minutes and serve the light salmon with the delicate leeks and a light drizzle of extra virgin olive oil.

Jamie Oliver started cooking in his parents' pub, The Cricketers, in Clavering, Essex, at the age of eight. He has since worked with some of the world's top chefs and is now running *Fifteen* – one of the best restaurants in London.

Jamie has written six bestselling cookery books that have sold over 11 million copies worldwide. His many award-winning television series have been sold in over 46 countries. He currently writes for *News of the World* in the UK, *Delicious* magazine in the UK and Australia, *Tip Culinair* magazine in Holland, *Ta Nea* in Greece, *Woman's Day* in Australia and *Taste* in South Africa.

He also started and continues to be involved with the charity *Fifteen Foundation*, which allows disadvantaged youngsters to follow their dreams and become chefs.

Jamie lives in London with his wife and two daughters.

Jamie Oliver
CRUNCHY THAI WRAPS

serves 8

1 carrot
1 red pepper
4 chillies
a bunch of chives
a bunch of coriander, roughly chopped
3 iceberg lettuces
a small bag of bean shoots
a small bag of bean sprouts
250g prawns
salt and freshly ground black pepper

for the dressing

a thumb-sized piece of ginger, peeled and grated
2 tablespoons soy sauce
1 tablespoon sesame oil
4 tablespoons olive oil
juice of 2 limes
2 teaspoons sesame seeds

Cut the carrot, pepper and chillies into fine matchsticks or, if you're strapped for time, just grate them. Mix in a bowl with the chives and coriander. Carefully remove the leaves from each iceberg lettuce, discarding any broken pieces. Mix the ingredients for the dressing together and drizzle over the top of the lettuce leaves. Then, using each lettuce leaf like a pancake place a handful of vegetables and a prawn into the middle of the leaf and fold it up (some people chop the prawns but I leave them whole). Season to taste and lay them snugly on a large plate. You can secure them with a cocktail stick if you like, but they should stay put. Alternatively, if your friends aren't too lazy, you could just prepare all the ingredients and let them wrap them up themselves.

Jamie Oliver
THAI WATERMELON SALAD

serves 4

¼ of a watermelon
2 handfuls of fresh coriander, leaves picked
2 handfuls of rocket
2 handfuls of fresh mint, leaves picked
a small bunch of radishes, finely sliced
a handful of peanuts or sunflower seeds
115g/4oz feta cheese

for the dressing

a thumb-sized piece of fresh ginger, peeled and grated
1 red, 1 yellow and 1 green chilli, deseeded and finely sliced
2 tablespoons soy sauce
6 tablespoons olive oil
1 teaspoon sesame oil
juice of 3–4 limes
sea salt and freshly ground black pepper

Remove the skin from the watermelon and cut the flesh into small cubes, removing as many seeds as you can be bothered to (but don't worry too much, as you can eat them and you'll hardly notice them in the salad).

When you pick the coriander leaves remove the stringier part of the stalks but keep the finer ones as they are nice to eat. Place in a bowl with the rocket, mint, watermelon and radishes. Put the ginger, chilli, soy sauce, olive oil and sesame oil into a smaller bowl and add just enough lime juice to cut through the oil – the number of limes you use will depend on how juicy they are. Season to taste and make sure the dressing is well-balanced.

Place your peanuts or sunflower seeds in the oven or in a pan and warm through, then roughly pound them up in a pestle and mortar or in a metal bowl using the end of a rolling-pin. Dress the salad really quickly. (You can use more dressing if you wish, but any left over is great to keep in the fridge to use the next day.) Divide between the plates, sprinkle over the hot peanuts or sunflower seeds and crumble the feta cheese over the top.

Warning: Do not give this dish to anyone without checking whether they are allergic to peanuts.

recipes © Jamie Oliver, photography © David Loftus
Thai Watermelon Salad extracted from *Jamie's Dinners* published by Michael Joseph / Penguin Books Ltd.

Lord David Owen
MOLL'S MARMALADE CAKE

This was my mother's most popular cake, and the recipe is still being used by my family (and even by Delia Smith).

8 oz (225g) self-raising flour, sifted
4 oz (110g) caster sugar
2 oz (50g) butter, at room temperature
2 oz (50g) lard, at room temperature
1 rounded tablespoon thick marmalade
Grated rind of half a large lemon
Grated rind of half a large orange
1 teaspoon mixed spice
1 teaspoon vinegar
a pinch of salt
6 fl oz (175ml) milk
4 oz (110g) mixed dried fruit
1 tablespoon demerara sugar

The Right
Honourable David Owen, Baron
Owen CH PC MD, British politician. In
1981 he was one of the founders of the
Social Democratic Party and was its leader
from 1983–1987, and of the reformed SDP
between 1988 and 1990.

Pre-heat the oven to Gas mark 4, 350°F (180°C)

Make this in a loaf tin with a base measurement of 7½ x 3 inches (19 cm x 8.5 cm), greased and base lined with lightly greased greaseproof paper.

First rub the butter and lard into the flour until crumbly then add the sugar, salt, mixed fruit, spice, lemon and orange rinds. Now stir in the milk a little at a time, add the vinegar and mix until the ingredients are well combined. Next stir in the marmalade and now the mixture should be of a good dropping consistency. Spoon the mixture into the prepared tin and spread it out evenly. Sprinkle the surface with demerara sugar and bake for 1–1¼ hours.

The cake, when cooked, will have shrunk away from the sides of the tin and the centre will be firm and springy to the touch. Leave the cake in its tin for 15 minutes then turn it out onto a wire cooling rack. When cold, store in an airtight tin.

Tara Palmer-Tomkinson
TARA P-T'S CHOCOLATE CRISPIES

50g butter
50g golden syrup
1 spoonful of Suchard Express (chocolate powder from Harvey Nicks) but Cadbury's if you can't find it.
Cornflakes

Melt the first 3 ingredients in a non stick saucepan then add then add cornflakes as required!

Put into cake cases.

Tara
Palmer-Tomkinson
is the famous British 'It Girl'.
She wrote a weekly column for
the *Sunday Times* and most recently
appeared in the British Television
series *I'm a Celebrity, Get Me
Out of Here!*

Sue Dicken

Tom Parker Bowles
SPICY SHEPHERD'S PIE

This adds a little Thai heat to an English classic. It might seem odd, but works wonderfully.

Serves 4

450g organic beef mince
2 medium red onions, coarsely chopped
3 small Thai chillies, finely chopped (de-seed and de-vein for less heat)
3 tablespoons of olive oil
1 can of beef consommé or equivalent amount of organic beef stock
a good few shakes of Tabasco
1 teaspoon of tomato purée
3 tablespoons of Worcestershire sauce
freshly ground pepper and salt
4 medium sized Maris Piper potatoes
generous lump of unsalted butter
splash of milk

Heat the olive oil and sweat the chillies to infuse in the oil for a couple of minutes. Add the onions and cook over a low heat until soft and brown (about 7 minutes). Turn up the heat a little and add the mince in handfuls, stirring into the onion. When all the onion and beef is mixed together and browned, add the tomato purée and mix until cooked, about a minute or so. After a minute, pour in the consommé or stock. Add the Worcestershire sauce and Tabasco and stir. Turn the heat down, simmer gently and reduce for about 30 minutes. Keep tasting to make sure it is ok. As this is reducing, peel the potatoes and throw into a large pan of cold, salted water. Bring to the boil and simmer until soft. Drain, put back in the pan and over the heat (to dry off any excess water). Add the butter, a splash of milk and mash. Put the mince into a shallow baking dish and cover with the potato. Dot the potato with chunks of butter, season with salt and pepper and put into the oven at 190°C / 375°F / Gas mark 5 for 25 minutes. Serve with peas or small broad beans, drenched in butter.

Tom Parker Bowles has a weekly column in *The Mail on Sunday* and each month in the *Tatler*. He has recently produced his first book *E is for Eating*.

Philip Pullman
OVER-INDULGENT PASTA

*I can't give quantities exactly because I measure by eye and hand. When I say
'enough for four' that might be enough for somebody else's six, or a greedy two.
Anyway, I think exact quantities are over-rated. Put in as much as you think will
taste right. If it doesn't taste right, adjust it next time you make it.*

pancetta – or smoked bacon – cut up into small chunks, enough to fill a cup or so.
asparagus – a dozen spears, or fewer, or more.
egg yolks – 4 or 6 – depends how greedy you are
Parmesan cheese
cream – you might as well
pasta of some biggish sort like penne, enough for four

Philip Pullman is the best-selling author of
the *His Dark Materials* trilogy of fantasy
novels, enjoyed by both children and adults.
The first volume of the trilogy, *Northern
Lights* won the Carnegie Medal for children's
fiction in 1995 and the last volume *The
Amber Spyglass* was awarded the Whitbread
Book of the Year prize in 2002, the first
children's book to receive that award. The
trilogy took third place in the BBC's *Big
Read* poll 2003.

Philip Pullman was awarded a CBE in the
New Year's Honour list in 2004.

Fry the pancetta or bacon slowly until it's not quite crisp. Meanwhile,
deal with the asparagus. The woody fibrous stuff near the bottom
is no good to anyone, so I peel it with a vegetable peeler. Cut
the stalks into chunks about as long as the middle joint of your
forefinger, or if you prefer, the top joint of your thumb. Boil them for
a couple of minutes and then drain them and add them to the bacon
in the frying pan.

While you're doing that, you might as well put the pasta on to cook.
It won't take long.

Put the egg yolks into a bowl and beat them up with as much cream as you feel your system
can absorb, and grind some pepper into it to take your mind off the cholesterol. Grate some
Parmesan cheese into it so that the cholesterol can fight back.

When the pasta is cooked, drain it and put it back into the saucepan. By this time the
bacon and asparagus should be just getting crisp. Dump the entire contents of the frying
pan in with the pasta, and scrape out all the delicious fat that came out of the bacon too.
Stir it about, and then add the beaten eggs and cream and stir them well in. The heat of the
pasta should cook the eggs slightly, and it will be unspeakably wonderful.

Paula Pryke
ICED STRAWBERRY PARFAIT
with MALIBU SALSA

Paula Pryke holds a
greatly influential position as one
of the most innovative florists in the world.
In addition to running her London shops, Paula
has written 7 books. She appears frequently on TV,
writes regular magazine columns and demonstrates
her floral design nationally and internationally.
She has run her world-renowned flower
school since 1994.

*This is a special summer dessert to make in advance. White
chocolate and coconut milk form the base of the parfait, which will
keep in the freezer for up to a month. All you need to do on the
day is chop up the fruit for the salsa.*

Ready in 30–40 minutes,
plus freezing time. Serves 8

For the Iced Parfait
400 ml can coconut milk
200g block white chocolate
200g strawberries, hulled
4 tablespoons icing sugar
284ml carton double cream
2 tablespoons Malibu

For the Salsa
3 tablespoons icing sugar
3 tablespoons Malibu
400g strawberries, hulled and chopped

1. For the parfait, tip the coconut milk into a small pan and break the chocolate. Warm gently over a low heat until the chocolate melts, then pour into a bowl and cool. Meanwhile lightly oil the inside of a 1kg loaf tin and line the base and sides with a large sheet of cling film.

2. Put 140g of the strawberries in a food processor with 2 tablespoons of the sugar and whizz together until puréed. Rub the purée through a sieve, then thinly slice the remaining strawberries. Whip the cream with remaining 2 tablespoons of sugar and the Malibu until it holds its shape, then fold into the coconut mixture with the strawberries and purée. Pour the mixture into the tin then freeze for 5 hours or until firm. (It will keep in the freezer for up to a month).

3. Up to 3 hours before serving the parfait, make the salsa. Mix the icing sugar and Malibu with the chopped strawberries and chill until ready to serve. Transfer the parfait to the fridge for 1 hour before serving. Tip out of the tin, strip away the cling film and cut into 8 thick slices. Serve with the salsa.

Pippa Rea
PIPPA'S MUSHROOM SOUP

Serves 4–6

1 oz (2 tablespoons) butter
1 small onion, finely chopped
1 tablespoon parsley finely chopped
3 tablespoons flour
½ teaspoon salt
½ teaspoon black pepper
¼ teaspoon dried oregano
¼ teaspoon cayenne pepper
850 ml (1½ pt) chicken stock. (285 ml (½ pt) of this can be milk)
1 lb mushrooms, (stalks removed) sliced
1 bay leaf
150 ml (5 fl oz) double cream
1 tablespoon lemon juice

Melt butter in a large saucepan.

Add onion and fry for 5 minutes until soft and translucent.

Remove from heat and add flour, salt, pepper, oregano, parsley and cayenne.

Mix into smooth paste.

Gradually stir in stock avoiding lumps.

Stir in the mushrooms and bay leaf.

Bring to boil, stirring constantly.

Reduce to low heat, cover and simmer for 30 mins.

Stir in cream and lemon juice for 2 mins.

Serve!

Pippa loved to entertain and have people round. She was a wonderful cook, although it was not her favourite pastime. This recipe for mushroom soup was one she often cooked, always tasted delicious and was lovely to have on those cold winter nights.

Vic Reeves
PICKLED EGG on a DOILY

Place a pickled egg on a doily and serve!!

Starter - 1 pickled egg on a doily

Main Course
     Sausage / Cabbage
Using a casserole dish :-

1 layer of Savoy Cabbage
     peppered and buttered

1 layer of Tolouse Sausages

repeat layers

cover with foil

cook in oven at 200°c for 1 hour.

Pudding

Sliced Mango with greek yoghurt

Yours faithfully
Vic Reeves

Vic Reeves
SAUSAGE & CABBAGE CASSEROLE

Serves 4

1 large Toulouse sausage (approx 500g)
1 savoy cabbage
butter
pepper

Using a casserole dish, put one layer of savoy cabbage, peppered and buttered in it. Add a layer of Toulouse sausage.

Repeat the layers.

Cover with foil.

Cook in oven at 200 °C / 400°F / Gas mark 6 for 1 hour.

SLICED MANGO with GREEK YOGHURT

1 mango, sliced
1 pot Greek yoghurt

Place the sliced mango in a bowl, cover with Greek yoghurt and serve.

The brilliant comedian and actor is well known for his double act with Bob Mortimer. He also played Marty Hopkirk in the BBC's 1990s revival of the comedy thriller *Randall and Hopkirk (Deceased)*.

Vic Reeves enjoys painting and is gaining a reputation as a successful artist.

In 2004 he was a contestant in the television series *I'm A Celebrity Get Me Out Of Here*.

He now hosts a show for Virgin Radio called *Vic Reeves' Big Night In* on Wednesdays and Thursdays at 7.00pm.

Sir Cliff Richard
PASTA with CHEESE & PEANUT SAUCE

Serves 1

30g (1 oz) uncooked pasta shells, bows or spirals
90g (3 oz) cauliflower florets
90g (3 oz) carrots, sliced

For the sauce

2 teaspoons low-fat spread
90g (3oz) button mushrooms, sliced
1 tablespoon crunchy peanut butter
60g (2 oz) curd cheese
4 tablespoons skimmed milk
salt and pepper
1 teaspoon finely chopped fresh parsley to garnish

Boil the pasta in boiling salted water according to the packaging instructions; drain and keep warm. Boil the cauliflower and carrots in salted water for about 8 minutes; drain and keep warm.

While the pasta and vegetables are cooking, make the sauce. Melt the low-fat spread over a low heat and stir-fry the mushrooms for 2–3 minutes. Mix together the peanut butter, curd cheese and milk, stir into the sliced mushrooms, season with salt and pepper, bring to the boil over a low heat, stirring all the time. Reduce the heat and simmer for 1–2 minutes.

Stir the pasta and vegetables into the sauce, transfer to a warm plate, sprinkle with parsley and serve with a mixed salad.

Sir Cliff is one of the UK's most popular singers. Over the last six decades he has charted more than 100 hit singles and has had a number one single in 1950s, 60s, 70s, 80s and 90s, from *Living Doll* to *The Millennium Prayer*. He was recently named the best selling rock/pop artist of all time in Britain.

Cliff was knighted in October 1995.

Joely Richardson
CHILLI MINCE TACO

extra virgin olive oil
1 large onion, finely chopped
sea salt and coarse ground black pepper
crushed chilli seeds
large portion of lean steak mince
1 red pepper, finely chopped
2 sticks of celery, finely chopped
1 large carrot, finely grated

Special Secret Sauce 'Homepride Chilli Con Carne Ready Made Sauce'.
I have tried and tested every Chilli sauce there is and this one is the best.

El Paso taco shells 1 or 2 packs
dips
salsa
guacamole
sour cream & chive
onion and garlic
shredded iceberg lettuce
cucumber – long thick strips
Irish mature Cheddar – grated

Heat oil in the pan, enough to cover the base of the pan and stir in the onions until lightly coloured. Meanwhile season the meat by adding plenty of salt and pepper together with 2 teaspoons of crushed chilli seeds – knead the meat with the seasoning so its all the way through the meat. Add the meat to the pan and cook till the meat turns light brown. Drain off any excess fat from the pan, but keeping some back to cook the rest of the ingredients.

Then add the red pepper, carrot and celery. Keep stirring making sure that all the colours are blending in and when cooking keep turning the sauce, breaking up the large pieces of meat so you get a nice even looking sauce.

Once you have cooked the vegetables and meat together for at least 20 minutes, add in the Homepride Sauce on a low heat for a good 30 – 45 minutes, keeping an eye on the sauce and stirring every so often.

Heat the oven and pop your Taco Shells in – cook according to the packet instructions.

Prepare table with your dips and salad. Once your Taco shells are cooked, place on the table, take your chilli off the heat and tuck in.

Joely Richardson
CHICKEN PASTA

Joely Richardson, successful British actress who appeared in her first film, *Charge of the Light Brigade*, at the age of three. Since then she has acted in numerous films and television dramas including: *101 Dalmations, Maybe Baby, The Patriot* and *The Affair of the Necklace*. In 2003, she took on the major role of playing Julia McNamara in the television drama *Nip/Tuck*.

Serves 4

1 pack Kerry Gold Irish Butter
1 large onion, finely chopped
4 chicken breasts diced
1 large pack of mushrooms sliced
1 large carton of double cream
1 pack of pasta bows
finely grated Parmesan cheese

Heat a quarter of the butter in a pan on a medium heat. Add the finely chopped onion until lightly browned and add the chicken until cooked.

Keep stirring the onions, chicken and butter, adding another quarter of the butter. Then add the mushrooms.

Cook the pasta in a separate saucepan. While the pasta is cooking, add the double cream slowly and keep stirring gently, simmering on a low heat for at least 20 minutes.

Serve the sauce on the pasta with some grated Parmesan cheese.

Mmmmmmmmmh

The Duchess of Richmond
CHOCOLATE BRANDY WHIP

This is my favourite recipe because it is quick in an emergency, extremely delicious, looks wonderful in small glasses or pots, and very easy to make.

Every good wish for the success of this appeal.

(no cooking needed)

110g (4 oz) plain chocolate
4 eggs
15g (½ oz) butter
1 tablespoon brandy
1 teaspoon hot water
a little vanilla essence
whipped cream (for garnish)

Cut up the chocolate and melt it in a basin over hot water. Remove from the heat. Separate eggs, beat yolks and add one at a time to the chocolate. Beat well after each addition until the mixture is soft and creamy. Add the hot water and vanilla essence.

Cut butter into small pieces and add them one at a time, beating until melted. Add brandy and leave mixture to cool.

Meanwhile whisk the egg whites until stiff. Fold into the mixture gently; do not beat, but continue folding until all the white disappears. Turn into a glass bowl or individual glasses. Top with cream.

Holly Riddle
VEGETABLE KADAI

Whilst travelling around India in 2004 Holly had a cookery lesson with a local chef learning about authentic spices and cooking methods. This curry is a stir-fry of fresh vegetables, cooked in a kadai (a large type of Indian wok) which are then coated in a gravy made from lots of spices, tomatoes and onions.

Holly had always planned to cook this meal for us, unfortunately she never got around to it, but I found her little book with its basic instructions and ingredients used, though not always the amounts needed! Thankfully there were many pictures in the book so my friend Emma and I counted cardamom, cloves and peppercorns and hoped that our guesswork would prove correct, we think it has. My family and I think it was an exceptionally tasty meal and wish we could have shared it with our darling Holly. There were some ingredients that I haven't been able to find readily in the shops, so, have omitted musk melon seeds (the seeds of the Galia melon) and black Cardamom, using all green instead.

Paneer is used to garnish this curry. It is an Indian cottage cheese, which can be made, if not available in the shops. I have included it in the recipe.

(continues over the page…)

113

Holly Riddle
VEGETABLE KADAI

serves 4

stage 1: the gravy

4 large onions, chopped **(300g)**
4 large tomatoes, chopped **(250g)**
water
5 whole cashews, crushed
8 green cardamom
3 black cardamom
2 bay leaves
1 star anise
1 large stick or bark of cinnamon broken into 2/3
½ teaspoon whole black peppercorns
6–8 cloves
4 cloves garlic, chopped
2.5cm fresh ginger, peeled and chopped
1 tablespoon olive oil or ghee
1 teaspoon turmeric
1 teaspoon ground cumin
1–2 teaspoons whole fenugreek
1 teaspoon ground coriander
1 teaspoon salt
1–2 teaspoons hot chilli powder

Place the onions and tomatoes in separate saucepans, cover with water and bring to the boil. Simmer over a medium heat until soft, approximately 20–25 minutes. Add more water if necessary. Once cooked, purée using a hand blender or liquidiser. Meanwhile grind the cashews in a pestle and mortar, set to one side. Using the same pestle and mortar, add the garlic and ginger and make a paste.

Heat a large skillet or frying pan then add oil or ghee. When hot add cardamom, bay leaves, star anise, cinnamon, peppercorns, garlic and ginger paste. Heat for 2-3 minutes until aromatic. Stir in tomato and onion until blended, then add turmeric, cumin, fenugreek, coriander, salt and chilli and cook gently for 5 minutes.

Next add the remaining spices and cook for another five minutes, stirring frequently. Finally add the ground cashews (and musk melon seeds if using). Once well blended either keep warm until vegetables are stir-fried, or better still cover and keep in a cold place overnight to develop the flavour.

1 large onion
2 large green peppers
4 large carrots
200g green beans
2 large tomatoes
5 tablespoons oil or 150g ghee
250ml double cream – more or less to taste
salt and pepper
sliced or chopped paneer to garnish
chopped fresh coriander to garnish

Wash, prepare and chop vegetables into bite sized chunks. The carrots can be julienned and the green beans sliced diagonally into three.

Heat a large wok or frying pan, add oil or ghee. Once hot, add onion, after a minute or two add the carrots, again cook for a minute before adding the peppers. Follow the same procedure for tomato and lastly the green beans.

Add gravy (gently reheat if made the day before), thoroughly coating the vegetables. Then add the cream, season with salt and pepper and cook over a gentle heat for approximately 5 minutes until the vegetables are tender or al dente, depending on preference.

Garnish with paneer and coriander. Serve with chapatis and / or rice.

paneer

3 litres full cream milk
90ml lemon juice or vinegar

Put the milk into a large saucepan and heat. Just before the milk boils add the lemon juice or vinegar, which will cause the milk to curdle.

Remove the pan from the heat. When the curds and whey have cooled a little, strain through a muslin cloth. Squeeze the curds into a ball using the muslin, then flatten under a weight for approximately two hours. (I placed the curds in their muslin cloth between two plates and used a heavy book as the weight). The paneer can now be sliced and used to garnish the curry.

Dame Anita Roddick
SCOTTISH HIGHLAND KICK

Quite the most sensational taste. Imagine a cold 2 hour walk in the Scottish hills to come into a kitchen where this soup is simmering on the cooker.

Serves 6

55g (2 oz) butter
30g (1 oz) plain flour
570ml (1 pint) milk
570ml (1 pint) chicken or veal stock
150ml (¼ pint) dry sherry
150ml (¼ pint) double cream
225g (8 oz) Stilton cheese, crumbled into small pieces
a pinch of salt and cayenne pepper
2 tablespoons flaked almonds, lightly toasted

1. Melt the butter in a large heavy saucepan, and stir in the flour. Cook the roux on a gentle heat for a moment or two without allowing it to colour. Add the milk gradually, stirring constantly, to make the smooth sauce (if you get any lumps briskly whisk the sauce with a small hand whisk – this should remove them).

2. Cook the sauce gently for about 5 minutes before adding the stock, sherry and cream.

3. Remove the soup from the heat, add the cheese and as soon as it has melted season to taste with salt and cayenne.

4. Serve soup hot (or dulled) with toasted almond flakes floating on each bowl, a nice chunk of fresh bread and discuss with friends / family the pleasure of taste.

Dame Anita Roddick is founder of The Body Shop, which opened in 1976. She is also well known for her campaigning work on environmental issues.

In 2003 Anita Roddick was created a Dame Commander of the British Empire.

Phillip Schofield
MY MUM'S POTATO CAKES

This is really quick, easy and cheap, but most of all delicious!

Mash as much potato as you like with salt, pepper, a little milk and butter. (The final consistency should be a little softer than normal mash…. but not over soft).

Wait until it is quite cool, then add a cup of self raising flour, if you only have plain, that'll do! It will still be a bit doughy and sticky, that's fine, but you will need a fair bit of flour on your hands to shape the mixture into balls. Put them on a baking tray and flatten down into circles about 1cm thick and 8cm round.

Put the baking tray at the top of a fairly hot oven 200°C / 425°F / Gas mark 7 and bake for 10–15 minutes, or until golden brown.

Serve them either hot or cold, spread with butter.

Mmmmmmmmmmmmm!

Phillip Schofield started his career on television presenting Children's BBC and the popular Saturday morning show *Going Live*. He was also a D.J. for Radio 1. In 1992 he turned to acting when he successfully took over the stage role of Joseph in *Joseph and the Amazing Technicolour Dreamcoat* from Jason Donovan. Then in 1998 he was the most amazing Doctor Doolittle in the theatre production of *Doctor Doolittle*.

He currently co-presents the ITV daytime show *This Morning*. He also presents the BBC nationwide quiz *Test the Nation* with Anne Robinson and the programme *Have I Been Here Before?*

Santa Sebag Montefiore
PANCAKES DE DULCE DE LECHE

Here are two recipes for you to choose from. When I lived out in Argentina as a nineteen year old, I grew fat on dulche de leche, which is the national obsession – you can buy it in jars in most supermarkets. It's made from milk and sugar and a little vanilla. Sounds easy to make oneself, but it's all about quantity, timing and magic. Every time I taste it I am transported back to that stunningly beautiful country. My first four novels are based in Argentina and Chile and they all feature dulche de leche very heavily. Thanks to me, the Argentine export industry is growing – and so am I, but not in the right places!

170g flour
20g sugar
a pinch of salt
3 eggs
2 egg yolks
85g butter
1½ cups warm milk
dulche de leche

Lightly beat all the products (not the dulce de leche) except the milk and the softened butter. Warm the milk but do not let it boil. Mix in the softened butter and let melt. Leave to rest for one hour. Butter very lightly a teflon crêpes pan and put in enough of the mixture to make a crêpe (thin but not too thin so the dulce de leche, which is heavy, does not brake them). Spread a thin layer of dulce de leche on each crepe and roll them up. Optional, add powdered sugar to decorate. Serve warm.

Santa Sebag Montefiore
DULCHE DE LECHE SOUFFLÉ

8 egg whites
8 egg yolks
1 large cup of dulce de leche
1 spoonful of sugar
soufflé dish

Butter and flour the soufflé dish and warm the oven to 200°C / 400°F / Gas mark 6.

Beat egg yolks with half the sugar until almost white.

Add the large cup of dulce de leche.

Mix well.

At the last moment beat the egg whites until stiff with the rest of the sugar.

Mix carefully and put in the soufflé dish.

Place in oven for only 10 minutes. The soufflé should rise well but be runny inside. That is why this soufflé should be made while everybody is eating the main course, as it has to be served inmediately.

Santa Montefiore is a bestselling international novelist, her books include: *Meet me Under the Ombu Tree* (2001), *The Butterfly Box* (2002) and her latest novel, *Last Voyage of the Valentina* (2005). Her next, *The Gypsy Madonna* is due to be published in March 2006.

Simon Sebag Montefiore
SEBAG'S SPECIAL MOROCCAN LENTIL SOUP

The story is about my family, the Sebags, who came from the beautiful seaside fortress-town of Essaouira on the Atlantic coast of Morrocco in the Mid-19th Century before becoming very Anglicised. When I went back there in search of my family history, I found there were still Sebags living there, and in Casablanca too, and this it turned out was one of the family dishes. In fact, I love it and after working hard on some Russian research, there is nothing more therapeutic than cooking up my thick and delicious and highly nutricious soup which takes such fifteen minutes to make. I MUST ADD too that I never cooked until recently, but after seven years of marriage with my wife Santa waiting for her to learn to cook, I finally realized it was never going to happen and I stopped grumbling. If I wanted some decent cooking, apart from pasta, I would have to learn myself. So this was the result and now I have learned other recipes too!! I have started to cook at last and I love it. It turns out even Santa likes my cooking, though she is somewhat surprised at my new enthusiasm, but then isn't life made for sudden enthusiasms?

Simon Sebag Montefiore is a Historian and author. His second book Stalin: The Court of the Red Tsar won the History Book of the Year Award at the British Book Awards 2004.

Put a tiny bit of oil in a pan until it is sizzling.

Chop up lots of onions, leeks, and whole garlics and cook up until they are browning, then add six fresh tomatoes, but puncture the skins so the juice lubricates the mix. When they too are sizzling, pour in three cups of water and let it boil.

Add a whole lemon's worth of lemon juice and then drop in the lemon.
Cut some ginger in slices and toss it in. Add, if you like it spicy, a light covering of paprika.

Then pour in a teacup of lentils (half a cup per person) and let it boil for fifteen minutes until you can see that the lentils are soft and speading.

Then stir and serve piping hot.

That is it.

sebag

Delia Smith
THAI GREEN CURRY with CHICKEN

This recipe is inspired by The Oriental's Cookery School in Bangkok. The unique flavours of Thai cooking are so simple and – because you can use a good-quality cooked chicken from the supermarket – this recipe is actually incredibly easy.
Serves 4-6

1 lb (450 g) cooked chicken, sliced into shreds
1½ tins (600ml) coconut milk

For the green curry paste:

8 green birds eye chillies (whole)
1 lemon grass stalk, sliced thinly and soaked for 30 minutes in 2 tablespoons lime juice
1 rounded teaspoon kaffir lime peel, pared and thinly shredded
7 thin slices Thai ginger (galangal)
1 heaped teaspoon coriander stalks, chopped
½ level teaspoon roasted ground cumin
½ level teaspoon roasted ground coriander
3 garlic cloves
5 Thai shallots peeled (or normal shallots if not available)
1 level teaspoon shrimp paste

For the finished sauce:

3-4 level dessertspoons Thai fish sauce
1 level teaspoon palm sugar
3 level dessertspoons fresh green peppercorns (or preserved in brine)
7 kaffir lime leaves
½ mild red chilli, de-seeded and cut into hair-like shreds
1 oz (25g) Thai basil leaves

You will also need a large flameproof casserole or a wok.

Delia Smith is a cookery Icon. She has sold over 17 million books and has single-handedly taught a nation to cook. She is Britain's best selling cookery author. Delia became a cookery writer for the *Daily Mirror* in 1969 and later for the *Evening Standard* in 1972, but she really came to the nation's attention when she started her cookery series *Family Fare* in 1973–1975. It was in 1995 that Delia's *Winter Collection* series started nationwide shortages of cranberries and in 1998 the publication of *Delia's How To Cook* and the accompanying TV series saw the sale of eggs and omelette pans soar! Delia's other passion is her beloved Norwich City Football Club where in 1999 she established Delia,s Canary Catering and there are now five successful restaurants.

The curry paste can be made well ahead of time and there's absolutely no work involved if you have a food processor or a liquidiser because all you do is simply pop all the curry paste ingredients in and whiz it to a paste (stopping once or twice to push the mixture back down from the sides on to the blades). In Thailand, of course, all these would be pounded by hand with a pestle and mortar, but food processors do cut out all the hard work.

What you need to end up with is a coarse paste but don't worry if it doesn't look very green – that's because I have cut the chilli content; in Thailand they use about 35! If you want yours to be green, then this is the answer! Your next task is to prepare all the rest of the ingredients.

To make the curry, first place the tins of coconut milk on a work surface, upside down. Then open them and inside you will see the whole thing has separated into thick cream and thin watery milk. Divide these by pouring the milk into one bowl and the cream into another. Next place a wok, without any oil in it, over a very high heat and then as soon as it becomes really hot, add three-quarters of the coconut cream. What you do now is literally fry it, stirring all the time so it doesn't catch. What will happen is it will start to separate, the oil will begin to seep out and it will reduce. Ignore the curdled look – this is normal. You may also like to note that when the cream begins to separate you can actually hear it give off a crackling noise. Next add the curry paste and three-quarters of the coconut milk, which should be added a little at a time, keeping the heat high and letting it reduce down slightly. Stay with it and keep stirring to prevent it sticking. Then add the Thai fish sauce and palm sugar, stir these in and then add the chicken pieces and the peppercorns. Stir again and simmer everything for about 4-5 minutes until the chicken is heated through. Then just before serving, place the lime leaves one on top of the other, roll them up tightly and slice them into very fine shreds. Then add them along with the red chilli and torn basil leaves. Serve with Thai fragrant rice.
NOTE: You can, if you like, freeze the leftover coconut milk and cream for use later on.

Spencer's Restaurant, Emsworth

LOIN of MONKFISH

stuffed with basil, sunblush tomato and mozzarella baked in olive oil and served on red pesto tagliatelle

Serves 4

4 x 375 g monkfish fillets – skinned & trimmed
8 thin slices pancetta
8 pieces sunblush tomato
250g mozzarella, sliced
8 large basil leaves

for the tagliatelle

250g fresh egg tagliatelle
125g sunblush tomato
60g roasted pine nuts
60ml olive oil
60g grated fresh parmesan
60ml double cream
flat leaf parsley to garnish

Pre-heat oven to 190°C / 370°F / gas mark 5
Slice open the monkfish fillets. Place 2 pieces of tomato, a slice of mozzarella and 2 basil leaves on each fillet. Close fillets back up.

Lay out 2 slices of pancetta and place monkfish fillet on top. Wrap pancetta around the fish. Repeat for each fillet. Place fish onto a roasting tray and drizzle with olive oil. Bake in the oven for 12-15 mins. Meanwhile boil a pan of water. Cook the tagliatelle in boiling water for 4 minutes and leave to drain.

For the pesto: Place the sunblush tomato, pine nuts, olive oil and grated parmesan into a food processor and blend until pureed.

Put the double cream into a large saucepan and bring to the boil. Add the red pesto and the cooked tagliatelle. Toss well.

To serve: Divide the tagliatelle between 4 plates. Slice each monkfish fillet into 3 pieces and arrange on top of the tagliatelle. Garnish with flat leaf parsley.

Juliet Stevenson
INFALLIBLE ICE CREAM

This is my mother in law's ice cream recipe – a foolproof substitute for Haagen Daz lovers who can't afford it all the time!

Serves 4

450g (1lb) frozen berries (raspberries, strawberries, blackberries)
2 tablespoons water
225g (8 oz) icing sugar
275ml (½ pint) whipping cream
juice ½ lemon

Put the fruit into a pan with the water. Cover and simmer very gently for 8-10 minutes until tender. Leave to cool. Sieve or mouli to remove pips and skin. Add icing sugar and lemon juice. Whip the cream until it hangs on the whisk. Fold into the cold puree. Turn into a container and leave in the freezer for 1 hour or until frozen for 1 inch round the edge. Turn into a bowl and beat with whisk or fork until smooth and creamy. Return to freezer until needed.

Juliet Stevenson, is an award-winning actress, who has worked extensively on stage, screen and radio.

Recent theatre work includes *We Happy Few* (Gieldgud), *The Country* (Royal Court), *Private Lives* (RNT) and she won the Laurence Olivier Best Actress award for her role in *Death and the Maiden* (Royal Court).

Her TV career began when she appeared in the TV serialisation of Catherine Cookson's novel *The Mallens*. In 1991 she played the part of Nina in the film *Truly, Madly, Deeply* and won the Evening Standard Film Award for Best Actress. Other films include *Pierpoint, Hear the Silence, The Politician's Wife* (nominated for Best Actress BAFTA), and *Cider with Rosie*.

Recent films include *Every Word is True, Being Julia, Mona Lisa Smile, Bend it Like Beckham* and *Emma*.

From 16 November Juliet returns to the stage in the title role of Tom Murphy's new play *Alice Trilogy* at the Jerwood Theatre Downstairs.

John Sullivan
PIE & MASH

My favourite traditional dish comes, like me, from South London. It is Pie and Mash, with the thick, green parsley sauce called " liquor".

pie & mash

1 onion, peeled and chopped
4oz mushrooms, wiped
2 sticks celery
2 medium sized carrots
1 sprig thyme
1 medium sized beef fillet
½ pint stock
parsley
4 sheets puff pastry
garlic
1 oyster (optional)
beaten egg

mash

4 medium potatoes
1 onion
butter or garlic oil

sauce

2 jellied eels
potato water
parsley

Heat a little of the garlic oil in a pan. Finely chop the vegetables and garlic and stir fry them in the oil. Dice three quarters of the beef fillet, slice the remaining quarter in thin strips and reserve.

Add the diced meat to the vegetables, add thyme and a little of the parsley, pour in the beef stock and reduce. Fry the beef strips in garlic oil.

Boil the potatoes in lightly salted water. When soft, drain and reserve the water. Mash the potatoes adding butter to taste. Caramelise a thinly sliced onion in butter and stir into the mashed potato.

Line each individual pie dish with a sheet of puff pastry and partly fill with the vegetables and meat mixture. Add a couple of the beef strips and an oyster, then another layer of pie filling.

Brush the rim of the pie with beaten egg and cover with a sheet of pastry for the lid. Trim the edges and decorate. Brush the top lightly with beaten egg.

Cook in a very hot oven for ten minutes.

Stir the eel jelly into the potato water add remaining parsley, stir and reduce.

Serve the pie with the potato, top with jellied eel and serve with the liquor.

John Sullivan OBE, is the man who gave us Del Boy Trotter, (Sir David Jason) Rodney the plonker (Nicholas Lyndhurst) and the rich and varied cast of *Only Fools and Horses*.

But "Fools" is only one of his successful comedy shows. His new series starring John Challis and Sue Holderness as Boycie and Marlene the car dealer and his wife from Hell, started this autumn.

John Sullivan lives in Surrey with his wife, Sharon. They have two sons and a daughter.

John Swannell

VENISON SAUSAGES
BRAISED IN RED WINE

My favourite recipe is Delia Smith's venison sausages braised in red wine

Serves 2–3

John Swannell is a leading portrait and
fashion photographer and prize-winning
television commercials director.

Bangers are bangers, but there are some bangers that are extremely
special – and venison sausages are positively five-star, especially
when you serve them braised slowly with herbs, shallots, mushrooms
and red wine. Then all you need is a dreamy pile of light, creamy
mashed potato to go with them.

1 lb (450g) venison sausages
1 dessertspoon olive oil
8 oz (225g) diced bacon or pancetta
1 large clove garlic, peeled
8 oz (225g) shallots, peeled
1 dessertspoon juniper berries
10 fl oz (275ml) red wine
1 teaspoon chopped fresh thyme
2 bay leaves
6 oz (175g) medium sized open cap mushrooms
1 heaped teaspoon plain flour
1 rounded teaspoon mustard powder
1 oz (25g) soft butter
1 rounded tablespoon redcurrant jelly
salt and freshly milled black pepper

First take a large flameproof casserole and heat the oil in it. Then, with the heat at a
medium, brown the sausages evenly all over, taking care not to split the skins by turning
them over too soon. Next, using a slotted spoon, transfer them to a plate while you brown
the diced bacon along with the garlic and shallots. Now crush the juniper berries very
slightly without breaking them - just enough to release their flavour. Return the sausages
to the casserole, pour in the wine and add the berries, then thyme and bay leaves. Now
season lightly, bring it all up to a gentle simmer, put a lid on the casserole, turn the heat as
low as possible and let it all simmer for 30 minutes.

After that, add the mushrooms, stirring them in well, then leave everything to cook gently for
a further 20 minutes – this time without the lid so the liquid reduces slightly. To finish off
remove the sausages and vegetables to a warm serving dish, mix the flour and the mustard
powder with the softened butter until you have a smooth paste and whisk this, a little at
a time, into the casserole. Let everything bubble for a few more minutes, then take the
casserole off the heat, return the sausages to the casserole, whisk in the redcurrant jelly
– and it's ready to serve.

Bangers and mash was a meal my mum used to make us as children - I thought then it was always special - then a few years ago I discovered Delia's recipe which, now that I am older and my palate more sophisticated, is worth all the extra time and effort involved, not to mention the time it takes to track down the Juniper berries (I could only ever find the dried variety)!

36 Inn on the Quay, Emsworth
PEAR, CHOCOLATE & FRANGIPAN STRUDEL with VANILLA ICE CREAM

Serves 4

frangipan

150g butter
15g sugar
150g ground almonds
3 tablespoons plain flour
3 eggs

Cream together the butter and sugar. Add the flour then the eggs – one at a time. Add the almonds and thoroughly mix.

poaching liquour

1 ltr water
500g sugar
1 lemon (zest + juice)
1 orance (zest + juice)
1 cinnamon stick
1 star anise
4 pears (peeled & cored)

Bring all ingredients up to the boil in a pot and simmer for 5 minutes. Place the pears in the stock and allow to simmer until tender.

1 kg puff pastry
200g plain chocolate chips
150g crushed, toasted hazelnuts

vanilla ice cream

1½ pt double cream
1 pt milk
3 vanilla pods
16 egg yolks
4 oz sugar

Bring milk, cream & vanilla pods to the boil. Whisk yolks and sugar together. Pour cream over and return to the heat for 8–10 minutes over a moderate heat. Strain and cool, then churn through an ice-cream machine.

Roll the puff pastry out to a dimension of 12 inches x 12 inches. Cut pears in half length ways.
Spoon the frangipan down one side of the puff pastry, leaving a 5 cm (2 inch) border.
Sprinkle half the quantity of hazelnuts and chocolate on the frangipan. Lay the pears on top then sprinkle the rest of the hazelnuts and chocolate on top of the pears.
Brush border with water, fold the puff pastry over and seal. Brush top with the egg wash.

Bake until golden at 180°C / 350°F / Gas mark 4 for approx 30–40 minutes.

Remove from oven and allow to sit for 10 minutes. Cut at an angle and serve with ice cream.

Alan Titchmarsh
LAMB CUTLETS SHREWSBURY

Serves 4   Time taken: 2 hours

8 Lamb cutlets
10g (½ oz) vegetable fat
110g (4 oz) button mushrooms
4 tablespoons redcurrant jelly
2 tablespoons Worcester Sauce
juice of 1 lemon
1 level tablespoons plain flour
¼ – ½ pint stock
salt and freshly ground pepper
pinch ground nutmeg
chopped parsley

Trim the excess fat from the cutlets. Heat the fat in a frying pan and brown the cutlets on both sides in the hot fat. Trim and slice the mushrooms.

After gaining a City and Guilds in horticulture, Alan went on to study at Oaklands in Hertfordshire for the National Certificate in Horticulture. He then gained the Kew Diploma after training at the Royal Botanic Gardens, Kew. He worked as a horticultural journalist for a number of publications, has written over 30 gardening books and several novels.

He won his first Gold Medal at the Chelsea Flower Show in 1985 for a country kitchen garden design.

Alan presented the BBC's lunchtime programme *Pebble Mill at One* for many years. He hosted the show *Gardener's World* between 1996 and 2002 and the popular *Ground Force* programme between 1997 and 2002.

His autobiography, *Trowel and Error* was published in 2002.

Remove the cutlets from the pan and place in a casserole dish with the mushrooms.

Measure the redcurrant jelly, Worcester Sauce and lemon juice into a saucepan. Stir over low heat until the jelly has melted and the ingredients are blended. (Stirring with a whisk often helps redcurrant jelly to soften.) Draw off the heat.

Add the flour to the hot fat remaining in the frying pan and if necessary, add extra to help absorb the flour. Stir over a low heat for about 10 minutes until golden brown. Stir in jelly mix and then sufficient stock to make a thick gravy. Bring to the boil stirring all the time to get smooth. Season with salt, pepper and nutmeg. Strain over the cutlets.

Cover and place in a moderate to slow oven 170°C / 325°F / Gas mark 3 and cook for 1½ hours.

Sprinkle with parsley and serve.

William Topley
PLANTER'S PUNCH

"Rum be sweet, Rum be sweet,
Doan leh dis drink
Sweep yuh orf yuh feet"

Rum was first produced in the seventeenth
century when it was known as 'Rumbullion'
or 'Kill Devil'. The drink known as 'Planters
Punch' may descend from the old Sangaree, and
there is a rhyme which goes

One of sour	*Pure lime juice*
Two of Sweet	*Sugar syrup*
Three of Strong	*Jamaican Rum*
Four of Weak	*Water and Ice*

To those basic ingredients add several dashes of aromatic bitters, then stir and pour over ice, adding some grated nutmeg on top. Decorate the glass with chunks of pineapple and place a hibiscus flower at the side to remind yourself of tropical verandas in the rain!

Ites passage!

William has been performing and writing music for 15 years, where he was the only Englishman on the *Lost Highway* label. He now records for Warner Brothers and has opened for *The Who*, *Simply Red* and *Mark Knopfler*, who plays on the latest album *Seafever*. He has also written lyrics for Steve Winwood and Sting's guitarist Dominic Miller, and has played more than 400 shows in the U.S.

Charlotte Uhlenbroek
THAI PRAWN NOODLES

Serves 4 Prep time 5 minutes

2 x 400g cans coconut milk
4 tablespoons Thai green curry paste
1 tablespoon Thai fish sauce
100g green beans, trimmed
1 red pepper, sliced
1 yellow pepper, sliced
400g medium raw prawns
zest and juice of 1 lime
6 tablespoons roughly chopped fresh coriander

Spoon the thick part of the coconut milk from both cans into a pan and heat through until it bubbles and becomes oily. Stir in the curry paste and cook for another minute until aromatic.

Dr Charlotte Uhlenbroek is a British zoologist and BBC television presenter.

Charlotte gained a BSc in Zoology and Psychology, followed by a PhD in Zoology at the University of Bristol. She then spent four years in the forests of Gombe, Tanzania, studying the communication of wild chimpanzees.

She presented the BBC 2 programme *Chimpanzee Diary* as part of the *Animal Zone* during 1998–99.

Pour the remaining coconut milk into the pan, stir in the fish sauce and bring to the boil. Simmer for three minutes, then add the green beans and simmer for another 2 minutes. Add the peppers and the prawns and simmer for another 3 minutes. Stir in the remaining ingredients and serve hot over cooked noodles.

(If using cooked prawns, add them at the last minute – just make sure they are piping hot.)

Great for last minute entertaining when surprise visitors arrive.

Carol Vorderman
PASTA with BROCCOLI & PINENUTS

Makes 4 servings

450g (1lb) broccoli
2 tablespoons (30ml) extra virgin olive oil
1 onion, chopped
2 garlic cloves, crushed
400g (14 oz) tinned chopped tomatoes
2 tablespoons (30ml) pine nuts
85g (3 oz) sultanas
350g (12 oz) non-wheat pasta
Low-sodium salt and freshly ground black pepper

Carol
is best known for
her work on the Channel 4 game
show *Countdown*, where she reveals her
intellectual ability by carrying out fast
and accurate mathematical
calculations as part of the game.
She was awarded an MBE
in June 2000.

Divide the broccoli into florets and briefly cook in a pan of boiling water for 3–4 minutes. Drain well and keep warm.

Heat the olive oil in a pan and cook the onion and garlic for 5 minutes until the onion is soft but not brown. Add the tomatoes and season with low-sodium salt and pepper and simmer for a few minutes. Add the broccoli and sultanas.

Toast the pine nuts in a dry pan for a minute or two until they start to turn golden.

Cook the pasta in a large pan of boiling water according to the directions on the packet. Drain and transfer to a serving dish. Mix with the broccoli mixture and the pine nuts.

Scatter with freshly grated Parmesan.

Recipe reproduced by courtesy of Virgin Books

134

Julie Walters
COCKLES

Mainly associated with comedy and character roles on both stage and screen, Julie won her first BAFTA for best actress in *Educating Rita* (1983). Since than she has played innumerable roles including the part of Molly Weasley in the *Harry Potter* series of films, in *Calendar Girls* and *Ahead of the Class*. She was awarded an OBE in 1999 for services to drama and has recently been appearing in the stage version of the comedy *Acorn Antiques*.

¼ pint fresh cockles
2 slices wholemeal bread
butter
freshly ground pepper

Butter the bread, place cockles on one piece, sprinkle with pepper, cover with the other piece.

Open mouth, shove in, clamp teeth down on bread and masticate – OK?

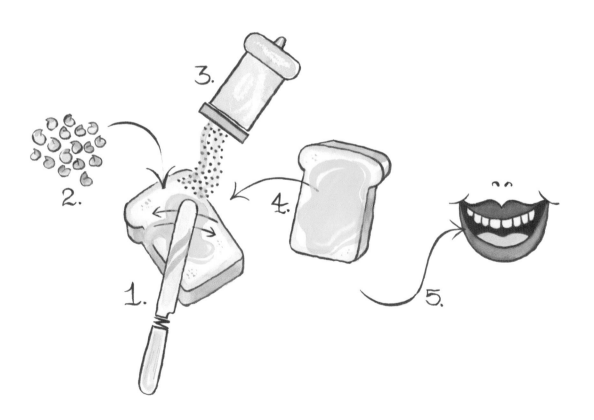

Richard Ward
CHEAT'S CHICKEN

Coming from a family of chefs, I am totally ashamed to admit to how useless a cook I truly am. But I learned this recipe from my chef Brother, when I needed something idiot-proof to 'entertain the Ladeees', and believe me, in my bachelor days, it came in very handy! They were all very impressed with my 'New Man, I Can Cook' approach and it worked wonders! Nowadays, I still sometimes make it for my wife as a treat, and even my children like it. I defy anybody not to be able to cook it without messing it up - I can do it and have still not mastered boiling an egg!

2 large lean chicken breasts
3 medium shallots
1 cup of sliced mushrooms
whipping cream – approx. 2 cups
Jerez sherry – 1 sherry glass full
olive oil for frying

Heat some olive oil in a non-stick wok. Chop shallots finely and fry until opaque. Cut chicken into small slices and pan fry until golden brown. Add sliced mushrooms and continue to fry until soft. Add a sherry glass full of sherry and cook until liquid is reduced by half. Add 2 cups of whipping cream and cook until the cream has reduced (thickened) to a creamy consistency.

Serve with Wild Rice, fine beans and a green side salad.

With exquisite cutting skills and a charming personality, Richard Ward is renowned for cornering the celebrity market and taking luxury hairdressing to the next level.

After 23 years in the business, Richard is the first to offer a unique zoned approach to the typical hair and beauty appointment. He has been nominated five times for the prestigious British Hairdresser of the Year Award and is a regular TV personality. Richard is firmly ensconced within the hairdressing elite and a true master of his trade.

David Willetts MP & Sarah Willetts
DELICIOUS PUDDING
(A recipe from New York 1920s)

7oz caster sugar
1½ oz butter
1 well rounded tablespoon plain flour
10oz milk
2 eggs
1 lemon juice and rind (you can add a second lemon juice and rind if you like it zesty!)

Preset oven to 150°C / 300°F / Gas mark 2.

Beat butter and sugar to cream. Add lemon juice , rind and all other ingredients – except egg whites. Beat and mix together. Don't worry if mixture curdles slightly. Beat egg whites to firm but not dry and fold lightly into lemon mixture.
Bake in greased soufflé dish set in a baking tray of cool water.

Cooking time about 45 minutes or when the surface of the pudding looks soft golden colour. The pudding separates into a soft spongy top with a creamy layer below.
If doubling add 2 cups of milk not 2½.

You can make this pudding the day before you eat it and gently warm it up – this takes the pressure off the big day when you have visitors. When the pudding is made and the table is set you can begin to breathe more easily!

It can be served with a red fruit salad.

A great friend of my grandmother's said "This is a delicious pudding, what is it called?" My grandmother replied "you've already said it – its called delicious pudding"

David Willetts is the Conservative Member of Parliament for Havant, which includes Emsworth. He currently serves as Shadow Secretary of State for Trade & Industry in the Shadow Cabinet, under Michael Howard. Previously he was Shadow Secretary of State for Work and Pensions.

Dr Rowan Williams, Archbishop of Canterbury
GINGER BISCUITS

Making these biscuits is a whole family enterprise, in which we all get very sticky and eat rather a lot of dough. The biscuits tend to vary in size rather dramatically depending on who made the dough ball.

Rowan Williams read Theology at Christ's College, Cambridge, he lectured at Mirfield Theological College and then from 1977, spent nine years in academic and parochial work in Cambridge. Dr. Williams was Professor of Theology at Oxford from 1986–1992, was enthroned as Bishop of Monmouth in 1992 and then as Archbishop of Wales in 2000. He was elected as Archbishop of Canterbury on 23 July 2002, and enthroned as the 104th Archbishop of Canterbury on 27 February 2003 In Canterbury Cathedral. Dr Williams is a Fellow of the British Academy.

110g (4 oz) margarine
350g (12 oz) self raising flour
175g (6 oz) granulated sugar
75g (3 oz) golden syrup (warmed)
1 egg
2 teaspoons of ground ginger
1 teaspoon of bicarbonate of soda

Cream the margarine and sugar together until well blended. Beat in the egg and the warm golden syrup. Stir the dry ingredients together and add gradually to the mixture. Roll into walnut sized balls and bake on a greased baking tray at 150°C / 300°F / Gas mark 2 for 10–15 minutes. Leave to cool on the tray.

Lorna Wing
PIMMS JELLY

Makes 6

Here's a summery Pimms Jelly recipe, deliciously easy to make. Feel free to change the mix of Pimms according to your favourite recipe as it won't make any difference as to how the jellies set. I like a combination of dry ginger and lemonade, but you can make it just with lemonade.

Do ahead. Make the jellies the day before. Store covered in the fridge.

275ml (10 fl oz) Pimms
200ml (7 fl oz) lemonade
275ml (10 fl oz) dry ginger ale
2 x 11.7g sachets Supercook gelatine
75g (3 oz) blueberries
75g (3 oz) raspberries
75g (3 oz) redcurrants, strings removed
6 strawberries, greenery removed, hulled and halved
6 sprigs borage or mint

Combine the Pimms, lemonade and ginger ale in a jug.

Heat 200ml (7 fl oz) of the Pimms mixture in a pan to just under boiling, then remove, sprinkle over the gelatine, leave to soak and soften for 5 minutes, then put back on a low heat and stir until dissolved. Do not boil. Add to the rest of the Pimms and stir well. Leave for a few minutes to allow the bubbles to subside, then remove the scum on the surface.

Divide the fruit between 6 x 225ml (8 fl oz) tumblers or bowls, top up with the Pimms and chill in the fridge for 3 hours until set. Poke in a sprig of borage or mint to decorate.

Famous for her amazing canapés, Lorna had her own catering company, whose client list was a 'Who's Who' of the rich and famous. Today she is a regular contributor to many food publications such as *The Sainsbury's Magazine.*

Terry Wogan
JACKET POTATO

There are a million and one ways to cook a potato, but this recipe is one of my family favourites.

Take one baking potato per person, put it in the microwave for five minutes or boil it whole until almost tender.

Then, with a sharp knife, cut in half lengthways and make a criss-cross pattern. Dribble some oil over, season with some salt and freshly ground black pepper, and to give it that extra 'something', add a dash of paprika. Bake them for 45 minutes at 200°C / 400°F / Gas mark 6 until nice and brown and crisp.

Enjoy!

A favourite Radio 2 presenter, Terry's *Wake Up To Wogan* programme attracts over 8 million listeners and is the most popular show on British radio.

Between 1985 and 1992 he hosted the popular *Wogan* television chat show three times a week.

The most listened to station in the UK

Trinny Woodall
CHOCOLATE BROWNIES

375g soft unsalted butter
375g best-quality dark chocolate
6 large eggs
1 tablespoon of vanilla extract
500g of caster sugar
225g of plain flour
1 tablespoon of salt
50g of white chocolate (roughly chopped)

Trinny Woodall
is co-host of the BBC style series
What Not To Wear

Preheat oven to 180°C / 350°F / Gas mark 4. Line your brownie pan – I think it's worth lining the sides as well as the base – with foil or parchment.

Melt the butter and chocolate together in a large, heavy-based pan. In a bowl or large wide mouthed measuring jug, beat the eggs with the sugar and vanilla. Measure the flour into another bowl and add the salt.

When the chocolate mixture is melted, let it cool a bit before beating in the eggs and sugar, and then the white chocolate and flour. Beat to combine smoothly and then scrape out of the saucepan into the lined pan.

Bake for about 25 minutes. When it's ready the top should be dried to a paler brown speckle, but the middle still dark and dense and gooey. Even with such a big batch, you need to keep alert, keep checking: the difference between gungy brownies and dry brownies is only a few minutes; remember that they will continue to cook as they cool.

Makes a maximum of 48.

Antony Worrall Thompson
THAI FISH CAKES

500g (1lb 2oz) fish fillets
half red pepper, chopped
2 red chillies, chopped
2 tablespoons coriander
3 spring onions, finely chopped
2 cloves garlic, chopped
1 stalk lemon grass, tender part only, chopped
1 tablespoon fish sauce
125ml (4 fl oz) coconut milk
1 whole egg
125g (4½oz) string beans
vegetable oil

1. Cut the fish into small pieces. Place the pepper, chillies, coriander, spring onions, garlic, lemon grass and fish sauce into food processor bowl and blend to a paste.

2. Add the fish pieces to the paste and blend well. Mix to a smooth paste with added coconut milk and egg.

3. Place the mixture in a bowl. Slice the beans finely into 3 mm and stir into fish paste. Chill in refrigerator overnight or for at least 2 hours.

4. Heat oil in the frying pan. Shape chilled paste into small patties with the help of a spoon. Fry in oil until crisp and brown, turning once. Drain on kitchen paper. Serve with Thai Dipping Sauce.

THAI DIPPING SAUCE

300ml/half a pint light soy sauce
2 tablespoons sesame oil
1 tablespoon honey
4 spring onions, diced
2 cloves garlic, finely chopped
2 chillies, finely shredded
2 teaspoons grated fresh ginger

1. Mix all the ingredients together.

Antony owns the popular restaurant *Notting Grill*.
He presents the popular *Saturday Kitchen* on
BBC2. He is a regular on *Ready Steady Cook*.
Antony has many books to his name, the latest
being *Real Family Food* published by Mitchell
Beazley. Antony is a regular judge for Academie
Culinaire's annual awards of excellence and until
recently was vice-chairman of the Restauranteurs
Association of Great Britain. He is passionate
about organic farming and his own range of food
products.

Antony Worrall Thompson
CHARGRILLED THAI BEEF SALAD

On my various trips to Thailand I have been impressed by the imaginative salads. This one is no exception. It has wonderful fresh flavours, and is perfect if you are on one of those perpetual diets.

Preparation and cooking: 40 minutes, plus marinating time   Serves 4

1 tablespoon jasmine rice, uncooked
2 dried red chillies
500g (1 lb 2 oz) thick fillet steak
2 tablespoons sesame oil
75 ml (2½ fl oz) kecap manis (sweet soy sauce)
2 teaspoons sugar
4 tablespoons lime juice
3 tablespoons Thai fish sauce
1 small cucumber, peeled, deseeded, halved lengthways and cut into 1 cm (¼ in) slices
4 red shallots, finely sliced
12 cherry tomatoes, halved
2 red chillies, finely sliced
1 handful fresh mint leaves
1 handful fresh coriander leaves
2 tablespoons fresh basil leaves, ripped
4 spring onions, finely sliced

1. Heat a dry frying pan, add the rice and toast until golden but not burnt. Grind the rice in a clean coffee-grinder or pound to a powder and set aside.

2. Reheat the frying pan and add the dried red chillies. Toast until they are smoky, then grind or pound to a powder and set aside.

3. Chargrill or pan-fry the beef for around 12 minutes, until well marked outside and rare to medium-rare inside. Place in a bowl and leave to rest for 10 minutes. Meanwhile, combine the sesame oil with the kecap manis and brush over the fillet. Marinate for 2 hours.

4. Dissolve the sugar in the lime juice and fish sauce. Combine half a teaspoon of the ground dried chilli powder with half a teaspoon of the ground rice and set aside. Combine the cucumber, shallots, cherry tomatoes, red chillies, herbs and spring onions in a large bowl. Add the lime juice and fish sauce mixture and toss to combine.

5. Slice the beef thinly. Toss the beef and ground rice, mix through the salad with any cooking juices that have collected in the beef bowl. Pile high on a large platter and serve with a salad of crunchy raw lettuce.

Kirsty Young
BANANA CAKE

175g (6oz) softened butter
85g (3oz) soft brown sugar
85g (3oz) caster sugar
3 eggs
175g (6oz) self raising flour
1 teaspoon vanilla essence
½ teaspoon fresh grated nutmeg
½ teaspoon ground cinnamon
1 ripe banana
½ cup of milk

to decorate

Demerara sugar
fresh grated nutmeg
ground cinnamon

Kirsty
is head news anchor
for British television channel Five
and was there for its launch in 1997.
Between 1999 and 2001 she worked for ITV on
ITV Lunchtime News, ITV Evening News
and *News at Ten*. She has also worked
for *Talk Radio*.

Preheat oven to 180°C / 350°F / Gas mark 4. Grease a round cake tin with removeable base. Beat together butter, sugar and eggs until light and fluffy. Sift in the flour and mix. In a separate bowl, mash together banana, milk, nutmeg, vanilla essence and cinnamon, and mix into the cake mixture. Pour the mixture into the cake tin and sprinkle with demerera sugar, nutmeg and cinnamon (and chopped nuts if more of a crunch is desired) and bake in the centre of the oven for 30 minutes or until golden and a skewer comes out clean.

Remove from tin and eat warm with a good cup of English tea!

Allwoods Wine Bar, Emsworth
GAZPACHO ANDALUZ

Serves 6

An ideal summertime starter or pre-starter.
For the 'wow' factor at your next barbeque why not try serving this in shot glasses
with a splash of iced vodka?!

500g over-ripe tomatoes
1 small stale ciabatta
1 green pepper
1 red pepper
1 yellow pepper
½ cucumber deseeded and peeled
¼ mild Spanish onion
½ clove garlic
4 dessert spoons of good quality red wine vinegar
pinch pepper
pinch salt
pinch cumin freshly ground
1 dessert spoon of sugar
250 mls of good quality olive oil
1 pint of iced water
1 dash of Tabasco

Place all ingredients (peppers de-seeded) raw and chopped into approximately 1 inch cubes in a bowl and mix with your hands. Chill overnight. The next day, blend thoroughly in a food processor and pass the chilled soup through a fine meshed sieve, or if you have one, a chinois. Check the consistency and seasoning, adjusting with a splash of cold water if necessary.

when we started this book...

... in January it was because we felt we wanted to do something, however small,
to raise money for the Tsunami victims in Khao Lak, Thailand. Our friends had
returned home from their holiday devastated by what they had been through
but determined to raise money for the people of Khao Lak and had asked for
fundraising ideas. We decided to try to collect some recipes, either Thai or favourite,
from celebrities and people who had become successful in their chosen career, put
them together and then sell locally. We were overwhelmed at the response from
such distinguished celebrities and soon realised we had a book on our hands.

The Paul Martin Design Company agreed to help us turn our recipes into the
book it is today, and we are so very grateful to *Paul Martin* and his design team; *Paul
Adams, Sue Dicken, Steve Hobbs, Rachel Parker, Jenny Ryan, Andrew Turner* and *Lavinia
Winch* who have generously given their time to this book.

We would like to take this opportunity to thank *Lord Richard Attenborough* for
writing the Foreword, all the Celebrities, their agents and PAs for sending us the
recipes and photographs, the local restaurants in Emsworth who have given recipes
and supported the appeal during the year, and the families of our friends who died
who have donated recipes.

Special thanks must go to *Lucy O'Donnell* at Lovedean Larder, producer of
OrgaSnic granola breakfast cereal and *Jenny Yeates* for their continued assistance
from the outset with this project.

We have had a great deal of help with all aspects of the book from collecting and testing the recipes to pre-order sales and owe a huge debt of gratitude to:

Joy Barden, Alison Bates, Ann Bates, Sophie Braithwaite, Sindy Caplan, Damien Carpanini, Robert Cooper, Simon and Helen Dear, Shirley Dumall, Lindsey Evans, Suzanna de Jong, Jenny de Jongh, Luca Del Bono, Annabel Elliot at Wild Card PR, Felicity Elmer, Juliana Foster, Honor Garrard, Sally Gordon, Melanie Grocott, Jenny Groves, Julia Harris, Jacqui Hepworth, Lynn Hill, Ghillie James, Gill Jefferies, Laura Jefferies, Paul Jefferies, Peter Knab, David Linnington, Barbie Lloyd, Sue Logan, Guy Lubbock, Sheila Marshall, Helena Michell Eden, Phillipa Morfitt at M+M Management, Joyce Murphy, Orlando Murrin, Tim O'Kelly, Gary Plaistow, Harry Pounds, Mark Povey, Sarah Randell, Floss Rodger, Debbie and Georgina Savage, Linda Shanks, Sue Slight, Steve Smith, Paula Sperring, Will Stretch, Karen Taylor, Lazlo Toth, Louise Townsend, Dee Warner, Claire Watts, Belinda White, Kate Wild, Jane Wilson, Lulu and Paul White, Jane Wood, Sally Yard.

If we have forgotten anyone we are really, really sorry.

Thank you for buying this book and enjoy!

Brigette Hardy *&* **Sarah Jefferies**

Brigette Hardy

There are few people in the world of food with Brigette's encyclopaedic knowledge of culinary practice and life-long dedication to getting the best the world has to offer onto the dinner plates of Britain. Brigette has an eye for the unusual and has an uncanny knack of spotting food fashion of the future. She has worked with many of the UK's top names in food manufacturing and the retail industry and currently balances a busy consultancy with her family life in Hampshire.

Sarah Jefferies

Sarah Jefferies trained as a Norland nursery nurse. In 1983 she set up a private day care nursery in Hampshire, which she is still running today. She is involved with children both professionally and voluntarily as Head of Welfare for Petersfield Youth Theatre.

Paul Martin

Paul Martin studied Graphic Design at The Royal College of Art, and after working in London set up his own design consultancy in Petersfield, Hampshire in 1984. The Paul Martin Design Company (www. pmdc.co.uk) produces effective, uniquely appropriate design solutions for its local, national and international clients.